A HALF CENTURY OF VIOLENCE IN TEXAS

The Bloody Legacy of Pink Higgins

by **Bill O'Neal**

EAKIN PRESS ⟡ Austin, Texas

For my friend and Higgins collaborator,
Bob Terry.

FIRST EDITION
Copyright © 1999
By Bill O'Neal
Published in the United States of America
By Eakin Press
A Division of Sunbelt Media, Inc.
P.O. Drawer 90159 ☜ Austin, Texas 78709-0159
email: eakinpub@sig.net
💻 website: www.eakinpress.com 💻

2 3 4 5 6 7 8 9

1-57168-304-6

Library of Congress Cataloging-in-Publication Data

O'Neal, Bill, 1942-
    The bloody legacy of Pink Higgins : A half century of violence in Texas /
by Bill O'Neal.
        p.   cm.
    Includes bibliographical references and index.
    ISBN 1-57168-304-6
    1. Higgins, John Calhoun Pinkney. 2. Pioneers—Texas—Biography. 3.
Violence—Texas—History—19th century. 4. Frontier and pioneer life—Texas. 5.
Texas—History—1846–1950. I. Title.
F391.H6054   1999
976.4'06—dc21   99-17586
                                                                        CIP

◉ **Contents** ◉

◦ Acknowledgments ◦

This book could not have been written without the diligent research and enthusiastic encouragement of Bob Terry. A great-great-nephew of Pink Higgins, Bob grew up in Roby, Texas, absorbing family stories from his father, Pink Terry, and from other Higgins descendants. In later years Bob began collecting documentary evidence, visiting the sites of various events, and performing other investigative activities. A few years ago Bob contacted me, offering to share his research if I would write a book centered around Pink Higgins. Bob knew that my great-grandfather, Jess Standard, had ridden for Pink, and he quickly intensified my longtime interest in the Horrell-Higgins feud and later events. Bob generously opened his files to me, toured me around various historic but lonely sites in West Texas, and in countless other ways made this book possible.

Also making significant contributions to this work were two great-grandchildren of Pink Higgins. Betty L. Giddens of Fort Worth patiently responded to my repeated requests for information, providing me with a wealth of materials she has compiled during a lifelong fascination with her family heritage. Dr. John T. Higgins of Lampasas graciously shared with me the results of his detailed investigations, as well as his carefully considered reflections about Pink and the activities which once wracked Lampasas County. Pink Higgins would have been deeply gratified at the pride and interest his descendants have taken in his life and character.

My mother, Jessie Standard O'Neal, is a native of Lampasas and was named for her grandfather, who cowboyed for Pink. She provided me with a great variety of useful materials about Lampasas, and regaled me with recollections of her grandfather and of descendants of Pink Higgins. My grandmother, Lucile Standard, shared her memories and photographic collection with me, particularly when I lived in Lampasas during the 1960s.

Jeff Jackson, an exceptionally resourceful local historian in Lampasas, generously permitted me to use documents he had discovered. Mark Langford, who owns the old Higgins ranch in northeast Lampasas County, courteously directed me to Higgins Mountain and Higgins Gap and other points of interest on his property. I received welcome assistance from the staff of the Lampasas Public Library, as well as from staff members at the Texas State Historical Association in Austin.

During the late 1980s I was privileged to associate with the preeminent Southwestern historian C. L. "Doc" Sonnichsen. Doc had investigated the Horrell-Higgins range war during the 1940s for his classic account of Texas feuds, *I'll Die Before I'll Run*. He related to me his sometimes tense experiences in Lampasas County, and I was proud to receive his approval of a paper I presented on the Horrell-Higgins troubles to a gathering in Tucson of the National Association for Outlaw-Lawman History.

For invaluable assistance in Snyder I am deeply grateful to my daughter and son-in-law, Berri and Heith Hodges. Heith is a native of Snyder, and on trips to his home, he and Berri have made numerous investigations on my behalf. At Snyder's Scurry County Museum, Berri located several photographs with the kind cooperation of curator Sue Goodwin. Over lunch

I was privileged to query Snyder's superb local historian, Aline Parks. Also in Snyder, my longtime friend, Jerry Worsham, provided fascinating background about the Johnson ranch house north of town.

At the Pioneer Museum in Sweetwater I was aided by Annette Mills, who entrusted me to copy and return photographs from the museum's impressive collection. For patiently responding to my questions I am indebted to Frank Hamer, Jr., of San Marcos, Kinnith Hardin of Rotan, and Pink Terry of Roby. In Post I was treated with gracious hospitality by community leader Giles McCrary.

At the Callahan County Courthouse in Baird, my search for trial documents was courteously facilitated by District Clerk Cubelle L. Harris and her deputy, Georgie Manion. At the Dawson County Courthouse in Lamesa, Deputy District Clerk Julie Vera cheerfully hunted trial information for me.

Librarian/archivist Christine Stopka expertly guided me through the holdings of the Texas Ranger Hall of Fame in Waco. In Stanton, Lora Bell Tom, assistant curator of the Martin County Historical Museum, shared her knowledge and memories of Our Lady of Mercy Academy, which was attended by two daughters of Pink Higgins. Jim Bradshaw, librarian/archivist of the Haley Library and History Center in Midland, expertly located an important interview by noted range historian J. Evetts Haley. The research staff at the Ector County Library in Odessa produced obscure information about Gee McMeans, while staff members of the Southwest Collection at Texas Tech University in Lubbock responded to every request for materials.

I owe a special debt of gratitude to Melissa Locke Roberts, gifted editor for Eakin Press, who has improved this and several other of my books with patience and meticulous expertise.

My wife, Karon, accompanied me on research trips, photographed numerous sites, worked with me at various research centers, and prepared the final manuscript. I could not have produced this book without her help and encouragement.

1

A Half Century of Higgins Violence

"The elder Higgins was quite a guy; there is no telling how many men he had killed during his lifetime."

Lena Hopson Powell about Pink Higgins

PINK HIGGINS WAS A GUNFIGHTER of the first rank. He participated in as many gunfights and killed as many adversaries as did celebrated shootists Wyatt Earp, Doc Holliday, Pat Garrett, Bat Masterson, John Ringo, and the Sundance Kid. Only a few gunfighters engaged in a greater number of deadly encounters than did Pink: Billy the Kid, Ben Thompson, Wild Bill Hickok, Wes Hardin, and Killin' Jim Miller, most of whose killings were assassinations.

Pink was not kill-crazy, like the psychotic Hardin, and he was not a problem drinker, like Holliday and Thompson and a host of other Westerners whose drinking bouts led to violent

1

altercations. Indeed, unique among front-rank shootists, Pink was a hard-working family man, the father of nine children who earned a living as a pioneer rancher, trail driver, and stock detective. But he was brought up on the Texas frontier, battling Comanches and rustlers and anyone else who challenged him. Like any prudent frontiersman, Pink was aggressive in defending himself and his interests. In order to survive on the frontier, a man had to have a strong sense of danger and a willingness to take direct action. Although Pink held firm moral and religious beliefs, he pragmatically regarded his killings as a necessity of frontier life. Like Wild Bill Hickok he wasted no time on regrets, and Pink would matter-of-factly describe his shootouts upon request.

During Pink's lifetime, it was generally assumed that he had killed fourteen men; some claimed that the total was eighteen. Exaggerating the number of gunfighter victims was commonplace across the West. Wes Hardin, for example, credited himself with more than forty fatalities, although at least half of these kills cannot be confirmed. For decades it was routinely stated that Billy the Kid killed twenty-one men, "one for each year of his life." He actually killed four men, while helping to gun down five more—admittedly an "impressive" total for a twenty-one-year-old. When Pink was asked, late in life, about his fourteen victims, he remarked, "I didn't kill all them men—but then again I got some that wasn't on the bill, so I guess it just about evens up."[1]

But it does not add up. Pink's number of even marginally confirmed kills does not total half the generally accepted number. Although he may have accounted for several unnamed victims while fighting Comanches and during an obscure shootout on the Mexican border, it is obvious that Pink Higgins was subject to the same exaggeration as all other noted gunfighters.

Wild Bill Hickok, the "Prince of Pistoleers," Billy the Kid, Wes Hardin, Ben Thompson, Longhair Jim Courtright, Luke Short, Jesse James, Cole Younger, Dallas Stoudenmire, and many other shootists relied primarily on pistols. Pink carried a handgun—as a young man, a cap-and-ball revolver, and later a .38 on a .44 frame. But he was a deadly rifle shot, and he always preferred to use a Winchester. When the action was close, instead of palming his revolver, Pink worked his Winchester rapid-fire, tripping the trigger with his thumb as he pulled back the lever.

Pink found it necessary to use his guns in self-defense from the time he was a teenager until he was in his fifties. Barely out of boyhood, he rode with older men to protect his exposed homeland against war parties; he killed rustlers with scornful abruptness; he stood up to opponents in deadly face-offs; and he led a faction in the Horrell-Higgins feud, Texas' bloodiest range war. During his last gunfight, when he was in his fifties, Pink killed his opponent with one shot in a classic *mano a mano* duel.

In between shootouts, Pink rode the range as a cowboy-rancher-stock detective. The cowboy reigns as the world's number-one folk hero, and the Western movies and novels that helped put him there also gave the gunfighter mythic status. Therefore, Pink's life of violent adventure on the cattle frontier would qualify him for mythic status on two counts to later generations. The fact that Pink Higgins is not as well-known as other legendary Westerners has little to do with the quantity of his deeds. But he was not murdered, like Wild Bill Hickok; he did not have a tragic flaw, like Doc Holliday; he was not killed at twenty-one, like Billy the Kid; he was never the subject of a charming movie, like Butch Cassidy and the Sundance Kid; and even though he fought in many gunfights, none of them were at Tombstone's OK Corral.

It is fascinating to chronicle a man of the West who repeatedly engaged in life-and-death encounters. But the violence did not end with Pink's uncharacteristically peaceful death, of a heart attack at the age of sixty-two in West Texas. Although Pink died in the second decade of the twentieth century, West Texas still embraced the values and attitudes of the frontier. West Texans continued to resort to violence as readily as frontiersmen of the 1800s, and juries retained the same pragmatic notions of self-defense as those of the nineteenth century. Although Pink reared his children to be law-abiding and productive citizens, the Higgins name would continue to be a magnet for violence.

After Pink's death, a new round of gunplay erupted, with tragic consequences for his family. These bloody events involved the region's greatest cattle baron, hired killers, no less a lawman than the legendary Frank Hamer, and Pink's eldest son, Judge Cullen Higgins. The action included deadly ambushes and wild street shootouts. But this final outburst of frontier violence has never before been examined in detail.

The story began with a pioneer family named Higgins . . .

2

Early Life of Pink Higgins

"Him no beef, him Comanche."

Tonkawa scout to Pink during pursuit
of Comanche raiders

PINK'S ANCESTORS WERE IRISH. During the 1700s, or perhaps as early as the 1600s, five members of the O'Higgins
family migrated from Ireland and settled in Maryland.[1]
Because of English subjugation over Ireland, Irish immigrants
sailed in large numbers for the American colonies. But English
immigrants and descendants made up most of the colonial
population, and they exhibited considerable prejudice and sus-
picion toward Irish Americans. Many Irish colonists, therefore, found it prudent to Americanize themselves by dropping
the *O'* from their last names and by leaving Catholicism for a
Protestant denomination. O'Higgins became Higgins, and these

5

former Irish Catholics became Baptists and Methodists, the most popular denominations on the American frontier.

As the Higgins family began to work its way west, the O'Higgins Irish blood was passed on from generation to generation. Ireland had been settled by Celts and Vikings and Normans, combative races who transmitted fighting qualities to the Irish. And Pink Higgins would become the embodiment of the classic fighting Irishman. The naturally bellicose tendencies of his Irish nature were heightened by the mortal dangers of life on the Texas frontier. Pink also would demonstrate other characteristics of his Irish ancestors: he had an affinity for horses, for example, and he was a natural storyteller, readily regaling those around him.

One of Pink's ancestors ventured from Maryland, where the most common occupation was tobacco farming, to the newly opened cotton lands of Mississippi. A son of this family, John Higgins, journeyed into northern Georgia as a Christian missionary to the Cherokees. The Cherokees were increasingly influenced by contact with white settlers, and there was considerable intermarriage between whites and these Indians. John Higgins, perhaps in part to facilitate his missionary efforts, married the daughter of a Cherokee chief. The Cherokee princess took the Americanized name of Mary Elizabeth.[2]

John and Mary Elizabeth Higgins became the parents of twelve children, including a son, John Holcomb Higgins, born on January 17, 1823. During the 1840s John Holcomb Higgins would marry a native of Spartanburg, South Carolina, Hester West, born on September 12, 1826. Hester's father was a prosperous horse breeder, and John Holcomb Higgins developed an interest in stock-raising.

John and Hester produced their first child, Mary, in 1847. Two years later another daughter, Julia, was born. Their first son came along on Friday, March 28, 1851, in Macon, Georgia. Following a custom of the day, John and Hester named their son after important public figures: John C. Calhoun, from South Carolina, who had died a year earlier

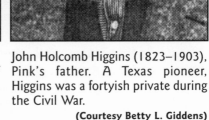

Mary Higgins, Pink's grandmother, was the daughter of a Cherokee chief in Georgia. She met John Higgins when he came to the Cherokees as a Christian missionary.

(Courtesy Betty L. Giddens)

John Holcomb Higgins (1823–1903), Pink's father. A Texas pioneer, Higgins was a fortyish private during the Civil War.

(Courtesy Betty L. Giddens)

after a notable career as a U.S. congressman and senator, cabinet member, and vice-president; and the Pinckney family from South Carolina, who had produced soldiers and governors and statesmen of national prominence. Of course, the infant boy's father and grandfather both were named John. So the newest Higgins baby was named John Calhoun Pinkney Higgins. The trio of surnames was commonplace for the times, but it all added up to an overwhelming label for a little boy. He would be known simply as "Pink."

Two more children were added to the family: Malinda, in 1854, and another son, in 1856. This younger son, like his older brother, was given a formidable name: Alberry W. Jackson Higgins. As with Pink, the family opted for an easier nickname, "Bud."

Bud (and possibly Malinda) was born in Texas, where the family had moved, probably in 1854. (Malinda Higgins was born on June 22, 1854—perhaps after the family reached Texas, because farmers often tried to arrive in time for spring planting.) Pink would have no memories of Georgia, because he was only three when the family migrated to Texas.

Texas was the fastest-growing state in the Union during the 1850s. The land was merely raw frontier when it was admitted as the twenty-eighth state in 1845. War with Mexico broke out in 1846, and when it ended two years later a tide of immigration swept toward the Lone Star State. Despite continuing border raids by *bandidos* and the terrible danger from Comanche and Kiowa war parties, settlers were drawn to the vast lands of Texas, with its favorable climate for raising crops and livestock. Cotton was king throughout the South in the 1850s, and Southern cotton farmers eagerly headed for Texas, often bringing slaves with them. In 1850 the population of Texas was 212,592, including 58,161 slaves; by the end of the decade those totals had approximately tripled, to 604,215, including 182,566 slaves.[3]

By 1854 a number of Georgia cotton farmers, many of whom were slaveholders, had contracted "Texas fever." A wagon train bound for Austin, the Texas state capital, was assembled in Atlanta, and John Holcomb Higgins was one of the Georgians who decided to move his family to the Lone State State. (Eventually all eleven of John's siblings moved to Texas, and some of them probably were members of the 1854 wagon train.) Pink was too young to remember the journey, but later his father reminisced "that there were thirty-six prairie schooners in the wagon train," and that more than one hundred slaves were among the party of travelers.[4]

More than eight hundred miles lay between Atlanta and Austin. The roads, especially in Texas, were merely rutted trails, impassable in wet weather, and the voyagers had to cross the mile-wide Mississippi, along with many lesser rivers. On the best days the wagon train would cover only about twenty miles, and so the entire journey would take at least two months.

Upon reaching Austin, some of the party settled at the state capital, while most of the other families took up land nearby in Travis County. The Georgians arrived in the middle of rapid population growth: Travis County grew from 3,138 in 1850 to 8,080 in 1860, while Austin jumped from 629 to 3,494 during the same period. The hills and dusty streets of Austin still displayed many log cabins, but there was an increasing number of frame houses and limestone commercial buildings, while a substantial Capitol and a lovely, white-columned Governor's Mansion were erected during the mid-1850s.

Higgins acquired land near Austin. The climate and rocky soil limited cotton farming; corn and wheat were the predominant crops in Travis County. But cattle, sheep, and horses were raised in large numbers, and John Higgins determined to go into cattle ranching. Needing more land, he decided to venture eighty miles northwest of Austin into northern Lampasas County, on the edge of the Texas frontier. It would have been easy to dispose of a farm in growing Travis County, while land was cheap in the Hill Country of exposed, newly organized Lampasas County.

When John Higgins moved his family in 1857, Lampasas County had been organized for only a year. The first permanent settlers camped in 1853 along Sulphur Creek, hoping to benefit from the medicinal qualities of the heavily mineralized waters. Other health-seekers soon came to "take the waters," and within a couple of years a village began to take shape just north of Sulphur Creek. The land had been granted to a Texas Revolutionary veteran, John Burleson, and when his daughters donated a townsite, the community was named Burleson. By 1855 there were "dry goods, groceries, and drug stores," along with "three boarding houses in addition to Scott's Cottage Hotel," to serve a steady parade of health-seekers. In that year 135 citizens petitioned the Texas Legislature for county status, and in the spring of 1856 Lampasas County was created. Burleson, renamed Lampasas, was designated the county seat. Lampasas was given a post office in 1857, but since no courthouse was erected a small frame building was rented for county business.[5]

John Higgins continued north from Lampasas to set up a ranch in the northeastern part of the county at the head of Beehouse Creek. The area featured rocky hills, and the valley between two large hills on the ranch became known as Higgins Gap. Ranch headquarters took shape at the westernmost of these hills, which was labeled Higgins Mountain. Nutritious grasses grew from the shallow, rocky soil, and there were open stands of live oak, mesquite, and juniper trees. The Colorado River formed the county's western border, the Lampasas River

Lampazos

The Lampasas River, which runs north to south through eastern Lampasas County, appears to have been named by Spaniards traveling through the region during the 1700s. The most likely discoverers of the river were scouts of the 1720 Aguayo Expedition, a force of 500 soldiers led by Governor Miguel de Aguayo from San Antonio to the vicinity of present-day Waco. Later there were other expeditions, associated with the establishment of Franciscan missions among various tribes of Texas Indians. Another Franciscan mission recently had been founded in the pueblo of Lampazos in the Mexican state of Nuevo Leon. Perhaps a priest or a soldier thought of Lampazos when naming the Texas river. Another possibility stems from the meaning of the Spanish word *lampazos*—"burdock," one of several plants with burs, large leaves, and a strong smell, which may have lined the riverbank. It also has been suggested that Lampasas derived from an Indian word for "water lily." Whether Indian or Spanish, the word was Americanized to "Lampasas."

ran through the eastern part of the county, and there were numerous spring-fed creeks.

Wildlife abounded in the sparsely settled frontier county. There were white-tailed deer, coyotes, beaver, game birds, and other fur-bearing animals. Herds of buffalo still grazed in the county, along with wild mustangs. The buffalo long had attracted Comanche hunters—who also were ferocious warriors.

For decades Comanches had retarded the western movement of Texas settlers, and the Higgins family would find them to be a deadly threat in Lampasas County. Comanches were superb horsemen, and used their mobility to pursue the buffalo that provided them with the essentials of life: food, tipis, winter robes, horn drinking cups, tools and arrowheads from bones, water bags from large intestines, and myriad other items. To hunt fleeing buffalo from horseback, Comanches used a lance and a short bow. Both weapons proved just as lethal against men as against buffalo.

A lance-wielding Comanche could ride down an opponent on foot, and a bow accoutered with a quiver that could hold a score of arrows was a devastating repeating weapon against a mounted adversary. Spanish muskets, American rifles, and horse pistols all were single-shot, muzzle-loading weapons. While their opponents were reloading, Comanches galloped to the attack, guiding their horses with their knees while firing arrow after arrow from close range. In the 1840s Texas Rangers, at last armed with their own repeating weapons, began to employ Colt revolvers from horseback. Although these cap-and-ball revolvers took several minutes to reload, Rangers carried at least two Colts apiece into combat, effectively battling Comanches in running fights. When the U.S. Army deployed across the Texas frontier following the war with Mexico, soldiers began to adopt the weapons and tactics of the Rangers. In 1849 a line of military outposts was built to protect the Texas frontier: Fort Gates (near present-day Gatesville) was established east of future Lampasas County, and Fort Croghan (near present-day Burnet) was constructed to the

Higgins Gap in northeastern Lampasas County. Higgins Mountain is on the left. **(Photo by Karon O'Neal)**

Higgins Mountain. Pink's home was nearby during most of his years in Lampasas County. **(Photo by Karon O'Neal)**

south. Within a few years, however, these posts were abandoned as the army built another line of forts farther to the west.

When John Higgins moved his family to Lampasas County, therefore, there was no nearby military presence, and fewer than 1,000 settlers. But Comanches continued to slip past the forts eastward into settled areas, riding into Lampasas County, among other places, in search of buffalo. And when Comanche hunters rode near isolated settlers, they became warriors. There were raids throughout the region, with horses stolen, cabins burned, children kidnapped, and settlers tortured, mutilated, killed, and scalped. Although the Lampasas Guards were organized on July 1, 1859, it was not enough for John Higgins. After two years of exposing himself, his wife and five children to mortal danger, Higgins felt it necessary to pull back to a safer locale.

In the fall of 1859, at the beginning of a bitter winter, the family moved two counties to the east.[7] Bell County was organized in 1850, and Belton (located on a stage route headed north from Austin) was the county seat. The western part of Bell County was hilly and rough, but there was good farmland to the east. By the time that John Higgins moved, the population of Bell County was nearly 5,000, including about 1,000 slaves.

During his boyhood on the Texas frontier Pink had little opportunity to go to school. His mother, a deeply religious "hard-shell Baptist," honed Pink's reading skills so that he could read the Bible. Indeed, the King James Bible was the principal textbook for countless children throughout the history of the American frontier. Instead of attending school, Pink helped his father, who had to rely early on his oldest son. As a youngster Pink learned to ride and then to break horses, to herd cattle, and to handle firearms. Boys grew up rapidly on the frontier, and like most pioneer fathers, John Higgins raised both his sons "to do a man's work at a very early age."[8] Eager to be considered a man, Pink learned to ride and shoot and hunt with the zest of a born outdoorsman.

After two and a half years in Bell County, John Higgins felt that, with the help of his oldest son, he could return to Lampasas County. Many people had fled the county, and there was plenty of grazing land for cattle, as well as mustangs to catch and break.

Pink was eleven in the spring of 1862 when the family moved back. Ironically, the Higgins family had left Lampasas County because of the threat of Comanche raiders, but when they returned in 1862—a year into the Civil War—the danger from war parties had worsened.

By the time the Civil War erupted in 1861, the combined efforts of the Texas Rangers and the U.S. Army at last had succeeded in sending the "Wild Tribes"—Comanches and Kiowas—into retreat. But when Texas seceded from the Union, the large contingent of Federal troops was withdrawn and the frontier forts were abandoned. Most of the Texas Rangers joined the Confederate Army (during the four-year Civil War

Pass the Corn Bread

The Higgins family, like most Texas frontier people of the 1850s and 1860s, ate a great deal of corn bread, salt pork, and sweet potatoes. Syrup was the primary sweetener, although if John Higgins was willing to rob a beehive, honey was available. Ranch people enjoyed strong coffee, but during the Civil War years the Union naval blockades made coffee virtually unavailable. Some Confederates brewed ersatz coffee with burned vegetables or blackened bread as grounds, but the Higgins family may have chosen to do without. Since the family lived in the countryside, milk and butter would have been available only when John Higgins kept a milch cow. Deer and other game abounded, so this ranch family probably enjoyed venison as well as beef.

approximately 60,000 of 92,000 Texas men between the ages of seventeen and forty-five served in a military unit). The Wild Tribes, quickly sensing the lack of resistance across the frontier, began to counterattack with murderous thrusts. Texas, the only Confederate state with a frontier exposed to Indian attack, assigned some of its native soldiers to fight Comanches and Kiowas instead of Yankees.

Maj. Ike M. Brown of the 27th Brigade, Texas State Troops, commanded detachments in Lampasas County and, just to the south, Burnet County. Most of the manpower for these frontier units came from the vicinity under protection. John Higgins, although nearly forty, enlisted as a private in the Second Regiment of the 27th Brigade.[9] Like Texas Rangers, these frontier soldiers were expected to provide their own weapons and horses. The men alternated between field duty and their homes: there was some patrolling of the countryside (one-fourth of the men were in the field at any given time); off-duty soldiers could protect their own families; and following a Comanche raid as many men as possible rode in hard pursuit.

Pvt. John Higgins certainly had ample opportunities to ride with pursuit parties. On April 11, 1862, shortly after Higgins moved back to Lampasas County, fifteen-year-old James Gracy was brutally slain by a war party west of the town of Lampasas, while a family of travelers at the site narrowly escaped a similar fate through a stout defense and a last-minute rescue.[10] Similar raids continued in the vicinity throughout the war years and beyond. Even after the war ended, the U.S. Army did not regarrison the Texas frontier. For the first two years of Reconstruction, Federal troops served as an occupation army in the settled portions of Texas. Frontier Texas, therefore, continued to be ravaged: from 1865 until 1867, 163 Texans were killed by Indians, another two dozen were wounded, and forty-three captured. By 1866 four out of five frontier ranches had been abandoned. In that year, since there was no military protection, Governor James W. Throckmorton and the Texas Legislature authorized a force of 1,000

Texas Rangers. But Reconstruction officials felt threatened by the idea of 1,000 armed Texans. The Texas Ranger force was disallowed, leaving frontier families to defend themselves. Even after Federal troops were assigned to the frontier in 1867, the line of forts was well to the west of Lampasas County, which continued to suffer from far-ranging raiding parties.

In 1865 C. C. Carter, who lived on the Lampasas River about sixteen miles north of town, was ambushed and fatally wounded by a war party. In 1868 a boy named Prince Ryan, while searching for a stray cow near Lampasas, was slain by warriors. About a year later a man named Patterson was killed in the countryside below Higgins Gap. Seven men from the neighborhood quickly gave pursuit. The posse caught up with the war party several miles to the east, killing three Indians without suffering any casualties themselves.[11]

In 1870 the entire region became "infested by large bodies of hostile Indians, evidently on the war path." Horses were stolen and at least one man was killed and "most horribly mutilated."[12] Two years later a war party stole several horses at night from a house a mile or so east of Lampasas. A cavalry detail was stationed in Lampasas, and the soldiers were quickly summoned. The Indians fled eastward down the road to Belton, and soon thirteen troopers and seven citizens rose in pursuit, with a Major Greene in command. The pursuit party caught up with the Indians after a chase of fifteen miles, but during the ensuing fight Major Greene was mortally wounded.[13]

The final Indian raid into Lampasas County occurred on February 13, 1874. The victim was Charles Peel, an Englishman who was intercepted by eight warriors in the northwestern part of the county. After a chase of about a mile, Peel, riddled with bullets, toppled from his horse. Distant witnesses buried the victim where he fell.[14]

And so it was that after the Higgins family moved back to Lampasas County in 1862, a dozen years of periodic Indian raids followed. Pink was a boy of eleven in 1862, and he was

"Killed & Skelped by Indians"

On April 10, 1862, fifteen-year-old James Gracy was sent from Lampasas to gather horses west of town. He spent the night at the cabin of Thomas Dawson, nine miles outside Lampasas. The next morning Gracy and thirteen-year-old John Stockman, who lived with Dawson, went out on foot to round up the horses.

A couple of miles from the cabin, Stockman ventured into a grove of scrub oaks to hunt a turkey. Suddenly, a party of about fifteen warriors appeared, driving a hundred or more stolen horses. Spotting Gracy, three warriors galloped to him, stripped off his clothes, and scalped him. Then they released him, but as Gracy raced away, they filled him with arrows and rifle balls.

Just as the Comanches were about to go after Stockman, a party from Austin blundered onto the scene. George Baker was astride a horse, while his wife, baby, and elderly father-in-law rode in a buggy. Several warriors stayed with their horse herd, but the others charged Baker and his family. Armed with a rifle and pistols, Baker covered a retreat to a thicket of timber and brush about two hundred yards away. Baker killed one warrior and wounded another, although he suffered several wounds himself. As the family found cover, the buggy horse bolted in the direction of Dawson's cabin, dragging the careening vehicle behind.

As a couple of warriors rode to capture the buggy horse, Dawson caught sight of the pursuit. He mounted one of his horses and galloped toward Lampasas for help. Within a mile of his home he encountered a four-man hunting party, who rode to the rescue and drove off the warriors. Baker recovered from his wounds after several weeks in bed, while Gracy was buried in Lampasas. His tombstone proclaimed: "Killed & Skelped by Indians."

almost twenty-three when the raids finally stopped. When Pvt. John Higgins was absent on military duty, young Pink was in charge of protecting his mother and sisters and little brother. Pink had become a crack shot. On the Texas frontier boys were taught to shoot and were given rifles at a young age. They grew into men early. Within a few years the tall, lanky teenager was riding with pursuit parties, which allowed his father to stay at home.

Pink was too young to enlist in any of the home guard companies that were organized during the Civil War—he was fourteen when the war ended—and his name is not listed on the muster roll of Company M of the "Minutemen" organized in Lampasas County in 1872. But for years he rode with informal pursuit posses, reporting that he "fought them all over the western part of Texas." During these combats he was wounded twice, once in the leg and once in the foot.[15]

Pursuit parties often used Tonkawas as trackers. Having been driven from their homelands by the ferocious Comanches, "Tonks" were eager to help white men hunt their longtime enemies. Tonkawas were known to be cannibals, but they ate the flesh of Comanches not for nourishment but to absorb the courage of the fierce warriors. Following one fight against Comanches, Pink broiled a piece of buffalo meat over coals. When a Tonkawa scout squatted before the fire with a piece of meat on a stick, Pink ordered, "Quit letting that greasy beef drip on my buffalo."[16]

"Him no beef," replied the Tonk. "Him Comanche."

Comanche raids across Texas subsided in the mid-1870s, following a large-scale army convergence on Comancheria during the Buffalo War of 1874–1875. Even before the Indian troubles ended, Pink was active in subduing stock thieves and other troublemakers. Like most other Southern men, Pink joined the Ku Klux Klan during the troubled Reconstruction years. Following the Civil War the KKK spread rapidly throughout the former Confederate states, as resentful Southerners secretly organized to defend themselves against victorious

Yankees and ex-slaves. But there had been few slaves in Lampasas County (ranchers seldom used slaves, since most work had to done from horseback, and a mounted slave could be expected to ride for freedom posthaste). The Census of 1860 tabulated a population of 1,028 in Lampasas County, with only about 150 slaves. Perhaps because of the organization of the Klan in Lampasas, as well as danger from Indians and a lack of economic opportunity, about half of the former slaves left the county following the Civil War. The few black families who remained did not challenge the white majority, and so there was little for the KKK to do in Lampasas County.

But a great need existed for concerted action against stock thieves and other outlaws. During the Civil War, army deserters congregated in frontier counties, subsisting on hunting and stealing, while establishing an atmosphere of general lawlessness. After the war a Law and Order League grew up across frontier Texas, somewhat after the fashion of the Ku Klux Klan elsewhere in the state. Like the KKK, the Law and Order League readily employed lynching. Also like the KKK, secret methods of communication were practiced by members. When encountering a stranger at night, for example, a Law and Order man would inquire, "Who comes?" If the moon was up, the correct reply was, "Moon down," and if the moon was down, the response was, "Moon up." A daytime encounter would begin with, "How may I know you?"—to which a fellow Law and Order man would say, "I'll word it with you." Then the two men would alternately call out the letters "D, N, R, S."[17]

While still a teenager Pink joined the Law and Order League, pursuing rustlers as readily as he pursued Comanche raiders. When he was eighteen, Pink and several other Law and Order men gave chase to a horse thief, doggedly following their prey for two days and two nights. Along the way, Law and Order supporters provided changes of mounts. When the rustler finally was overtaken, the tired pursuers decided to apply summary justice. A rope was thrown over the limb of a hackberry tree, and Pink adjusted the noose around the captive's neck. Given an opportunity to speak, the rustler gamely allowed that he knew he was going to hell, and that he wanted to arrive in time to find a partner for the first dance. Then he kicked his horse out from under himself and commenced his final journey.[18]

As a teenaged member of the Law and Order League, Pink launched a personal campaign against rustlers that he would maintain for the rest of his life. From boyhood Pink raised cattle and horses with his father, and he was hardly out of adolescence when he began acquiring his own livestock. Rustlers who posed a personal threat to Pink and his property would find that they had incurred the enmity of a very dangerous man.

Rustling was an inevitable part of frontier ranching, and rustling grew with the spectacular expansion of the Western cattle industry after the Civil War. Pink Higgins, a product of the Texas frontier, eagerly became part of the greatest Western adventure of that era. Following the Civil War, cattle herds were driven out of Texas to railheads in Kansas and elsewhere. The American public was captivated by cowboys, the colorful "knights of the range" who rode horseback and twirled lariats and wore boots, spurs, chaps, bandannas, and big hats. Countless boys yearned to run away to Texas and become cowboys. Pink lived on the Texas frontier, and he had grown up riding and roping and chasing longhorns. In 1868, just turned seventeen but tall and adventurous, Pink helped trail a herd to Wyoming.

The drive was put together by Perry Townsen, one of Lampasas County's first settlers. A native of Tennessee, Townsen began ranching near the Lampasas River in 1854, and later he built Townsen's Mill north of the Higgins ranch. Townsen trailed a cattle herd to Fort Sumner, New Mexico, in 1866, and the next year he led a drive all the way to Montana. For his 1868 crew, Townsen enlisted relatives and in-laws— John and Bill Townsen, Tom Stanley, Bob Mitchell—as well as his young neighbor, Pink Higgins.[19]

Perry Townsen's 1868 drive was a pioneering venture to

a distant part of the frontier. Cattle ranges had just opened in southern Wyoming. Cheyenne was founded when the Union Pacific Railroad built westward across southern Wyoming in the summer of 1867. John Wesley Iliff, the "Cattle King of the Plains," aggressively pursued railroad and military beef contracts. Iliff ranged his cattle along the South Platte River in northeastern Colorado, and in 1866, when partners Charles Goodnight and Oliver Loving drove their first herd into Colorado, Iliff bought 800 head of longhorns from them. (Loving was killed by Indians the next year.) In 1868 Iliff purchased a herd from Goodnight for delivery to Cheyenne. With Iliff, Goodnight, and other cattlemen rapidly acquiring beef contracts, longhorns were driven to southern Wyoming ranges by the thousands. Seventeen-year-old Pink Higgins helped drive one of the first herds of longhorns into Wyoming in 1868, riding along the Goodnight-Loving Trail across West Texas, New Mexico, and Colorado.

In 1866 Goodnight and Loving had angled southwestward from Fort Belknap, north of Lampasas County on the Brazos River, to the Pecos River. When Pink made his first long drive in 1868, the herd (which may have included some of John Higgins' cattle) probably was trailed northwestward along the Colorado River until intersecting the Goodnight-Loving Trail. (It is likely that Perry Townsen had followed this route the previous two years.) The last eighty miles to the Pecos included nothing but harsh, dry terrain.

Before setting out on this stretch the herd was rested and watered, then driven at night and the next day. During the second night the thirsty longhorns began to smell water, and after reaching the Horsehead Crossing of the Pecos they were rested again. The drive next followed the river northwestward into New Mexico, then north along the Pecos toward Colorado. Goodnight had blazed his trail into Colorado through Trinchera Pass, then continued east of the Rocky Mountains. The route led across the Arkansas River, passed east of Denver, and crossed the South Platte before finally entering Wyoming.

For most of the 1,100-mile trek there was good water and grass, and Pink learned that if the hardy longhorns were shoved slowly up the trail, they could actually gain weight during a drive. Trail-driving was hard, dusty work. Breakfast was before dawn, so that the crew was in the saddle by first light. Working in pairs, the cowboys also put in a couple of hours of night herding, trying to keep the snuffy longhorns bedded down. During the day most of the crew—almost certainly including the teenaged rookie, Pink Higgins—rode drag, pushing the herd from behind. Drag riders ate dust all day; bandannas pulled over the nose filtered some of the dust, but clothing and skin became thick with grime. Pink and the other drovers were assigned a "string" of horses, riding two each day while the other animals rested. The steadiest mount from each string was saddled at nightfall, for use in riding night herd and, if necessary, during stampedes. At the end of a drive, drovers, who earned about one dollar a day, were paid off.

When Pink returned from the long drive to Wyoming, he was an experienced trail driver with the ambition to lead his own herds. Two years later Pink and Bob Mitchell helped Jasper Townsen, Perry's nephew, drive a small herd to Calvert, about eighty miles east of Lampasas. In 1871 Pink was part of a group which bought 900 head of yearling steers at fifty cents per head, and in 1872 they purchased 1,700 more yearling steers at one dollar per head. The next year, Pink, Jasper Townsen, and Bob, Ben and Alonzo Mitchell, among others, drove this herd up the newly opened Western Trail, past Fort Griffin and Fort Belknap to Doan's Store on the Red River. After crossing the Red, the trail led north through western Oklahoma, then into western Kansas, where the Santa Fe Railroad was laying track. This large herd was more than four months on the trail, allowing ample time for the cattle to graze. En route there were "some thrilling experiences with the Indians," perhaps the last time Pink went to battle against warriors. It was late July before the herd finally reached Dodge.[20]

Pink Higgins as a young man. From a cracked tintype.

(Courtesy Betty L. Giddens)

Dodge City was founded along the Santa Fe Railroad in 1872 and became a shipping point for buffalo hides, but cattle pens were not built at Dodge until 1876. In 1871 an estimated 300,000 to 600,000 cattle unsold at Ellsworth and Abilene were brought to the open range of western Kansas to be nearer these markets. But the winter of 1871–1872 was so vicious that as many as 200,000 head died. The Kansas market therefore was excellent in 1872, and there were more ready buyers the next year when the big Lampasas County herd was driven north. The two-year-olds sold for eight dollars apiece.[21] Pink was only twenty-two, but this was the greatest success he would ever enjoy in the range cattle business.

Pink next drove a herd to the Kansas City stockyards,[22] heading east until intersecting the Chisholm Trail. At Fort Worth the herd left the Chisholm Trail, moving northeast to the old Shawnee Trail. After crossing the Red River the Shawnee angled northeast across eastern Oklahoma to Baxter Springs in the southeastern corner of Kansas. From Baxter Springs the trail headed north another 170 miles to Kansas City.

Now a successful trail boss, Pink would be employed in the future to lead other drives. While not on the trail, Pink would spend a great deal of time in the saddle, buying and selling and trading cattle. He did interrupt his activities as a cattleman long enough to take a wife. On January 1, 1875, Pink married Betty Mitchell May, who had a sad background. Born Delilah Elizabeth Mitchell in Tennessee, she was called "Betty." A contingent of Mitchells moved by wagon train to Lampasas County, but Betty's parents died en route. She continued on with the rest of the family, who settled in northeastern Lampasas County, not far from Higgins Gap. The leader of the family now was Betty's uncle, Mack Mitchell, who built a cattle ranch and reared his brother's orphaned children along with his own. Betty's grandmother, Elizabeth Wren Mitchell, also accompanied the wagon train from Tennessee and lived at the family ranch.[23]

Pink Higgins knew his neighbors well, and rode on trail

drives with the Mitchell brothers. Pink also became close to another family member, Bill Wren. Betty Mitchell previously had married a man named May. They had a daughter, Ida, but May died in November 1871. A little over three years later, Betty and Pink were married. Within the year, on December 1, 1875, Betty gave birth to their first child, Cullen. By the time Betty became pregnant again, Pink was embroiled in a deadly range war—the Horrell-Higgins feud.

3

The Horrell
Brothers

"Well, I raised my boys to be fighters."

Mrs. Elizabeth Horrell about her sons

THE HORRELL AND HIGGINS FAMILIES came to Lampasas County in the same year, 1857. Benedict Horrell, sixty-six in 1857, had been farming in Arkansas since the late 1830s, and he brought his third wife, a twenty-two-year-old son, and three daughters to Texas. Another Horrell household on the trek from Arkansas was headed by Sam, Benedict's oldest son. In 1857 Sam Horrell was thirty-seven, and his wife Elizabeth was three years younger. Sam and Elizabeth were the parents of seven boys and an infant daughter: Bill, eighteen; John, sixteen; Sam, Jr., fourteen; Mart, eleven; Tom, nine; Ben, six;

26

Merritt, three; and baby Sally. The family settled about ten miles northeast of Lampasas.[1]

"All of the boys were rather sociable and easy to get acquainted with," recalled a neighbor, John Nichols. But he added that they were "very clannish." Although the brothers were competitive and sometimes scrapped with each other, they learned to rally to any family member with fists or guns. "Well," observed Elizabeth Horrell with the pride of a frontier mother, "I raised my boys to be fighters."[2]

Her oldest son, Bill Horrell, went off to fight in the Civil War, but he died of illness while in Confederate service. Sam Horrell, who had enlisted in the Lampasas Guards during the Indian alarms of 1859, also served in home guard units during the war, and so did his next oldest sons, John and Sam, Jr. During the war Sam moved his family to a more promising range in the northeastern part of the county, not far from Higgins Gap.

Also during the war the boys began to marry. John, Mart, and Ben wed Grizzell sisters. When the wives of Sam and Mart had a falling out, "Mart was going to whip Sam over it," according to John Nichols. "Mart was rather surly at times," explained Nichols. "When a quarrel started he did not want to waste any words but wanted to go straight to business." When he went straight at his brother, though, Sam clubbed him with his revolver, and Sam, Sr., intervened to settle down the feisty Mart.[3]

In 1868 the family decided to round up their cattle and move to California. When the Horrell party reached Las Cruces, New Mexico, they had an opportunity to sell the herd. But John, acting as trail boss, was shot to death in camp by a drover who claimed he had not been paid. Not long afterward, in January 1869, John's widow, Sallie Ann, her three children, twenty-year-old Tom, and forty-eight-year-old Sam were attacked by Apache warriors. The Horrells were jumped at San Augustine Pass, about twenty miles northeast of Las Cruces. Sam Horrell was killed outright, but Sallie Ann picked up his revolver, flattened the three children on the bottom of their wagon, and helped Tom fight off the war party.[4]

With Sam and John dead, and without cattle to drive, the family decided to return to Lampasas County. The two widows settled at Lampasas; Elizabeth found a house near the town square, while Sallie Ann moved onto property owned by John near the medicinal springs, renting space to health-seeking campers. Tom began ranching on Mesquite Creek a few miles east of town. At sixteen, Ben married a fifteen-year-old, and Merritt married when he was nineteen. The Horrells had to rebuild their herds from scratch, and perhaps it was during this period that some of the boys began swinging a wide loop.

When Comanche depredations triggered the organization of a minuteman company in August 1872, Tom, Mart, Merritt, Ben, and their brother-in-law, Bill Bowen, enlisted. "All of them were a little better than average shots," pointed out John Nichols. Tom Horrell was appointed corporal of the twenty-man unit, which soon disbanded. Although slightly cross-eyed, Tom "was the smartest of them all," declared Nichols. The "general" of the brothers, Tom "was a natural diplomat, suave, polite, gushing and talkative when he met you." Fair-haired with a florid complexion, like all of the brothers, Tom was 5'9 and weighed about 165 pounds. The pugnacious Mart was the same size, while Merritt was smaller, no more than 140 pounds. None of the brothers played cards or gambled on anything other than an occasional horse race, but they were fond of carousing in Lampasas saloons. "They drank considerable," said Nichols, adding ominously that "they were always loaded for bear, drunk or sober."[5]

These characteristics inevitably led to trouble. At midday on Tuesday, January 14, 1873, Sheriff S. T. Denson tried to arrest Mark Short, who was creating a drunken disturbance in a saloon. But Wash Short backed up his brother, and in the ensuing struggle the sheriff was wounded. Tom Sparks, brother-in-law of the injured lawman, and several other citizens hurried to offer help. Tom, Mart, and Ben Horrell blocked their path so that the Short brothers—fellow saloon denizens—could escape. Sparks quickly mounted a posse, but the Horrells already had jumped on their horses. The Horrell brothers again blocked the pursuers, threatening to fight, while the Shorts galloped to safety.[6]

Frustrated over the wounding of their sheriff, the flagrant support of the Shorts by the Horrells, and the general lawlessness, county officials sent a request for help to Governor E. J. Davis. Davis was a Republican and a former Union officer who was handed the governorship by Reconstruction officials through the obviously fraudulent election of 1869. Among the numerous controversial actions of Governor Davis was the creation of the 250-man State Police. Forty percent of the force was composed of former slaves, and members of the State Police were as despised as the Union occupation troops. But Sgt. J. M. Redmon and a detail of the State Police, responding to the request for assistance, made the two-day ride from Austin in mid-February 1873, intending to make numerous arrests. Lampasas County citizens offered haven to the fugitives, however, and regularly discharged firearms during the middle of the night to defy the detested State Police. After several days, Sergeant Redmon led his men back to Austin, empty-handed.

Angrily, the Texas adjutant general and chief of state police, F. L. Britton, ordered another detachment to Lampasas. The detail was commanded by Britton's brother-in-law, State Police Capt. T. W. Williams, who was directed to ban the use of firearms in Lampasas and to make key arrests. On the road to Lampasas from Austin, Captain Williams, who had been drinking throughout the day, remarked to a passerby that he intended "to clean up those damned Horrell boys."[7]

Williams led his men into Lampasas on Friday afternoon, March 14, 1873. As the policemen tied their horses to live oak trees clustered in the town square, Williams saw a man who was wearing a revolver enter a saloon. The armed man was Bill Bowen, brother-in-law of the Horrells, and the saloon he entered was the favorite haunt of the brothers and their friends. Jerry Scott's Matador Saloon was on the west side of the square, the second door from the northwest corner. Williams left a black officer and two other men with the horses, and took three policemen with him into the saloon.

Mart, Tom, and Merritt Horrell, along with brothers-in-law Bill Bowen, Ben Turner and Jim Grizzell, the Short brothers, and at least ten other cowboys, were lounging inside Scott's establishment. A game of billiards was under way and in one corner a fiddle and a banjo provided music, but all eyes suspiciously shifted to the lawmen as they entered.

Williams approached the bar, ordered drinks, and then boldly addressed Bowen. "I believe you have a six-shooter," he said, nodding at Bowen's holstered revolver. "I arrest you."

"Bill," snapped the pugnacious Mart Horrell, "you have done nothing and need not be arrested if you don't want to."[8]

Williams responded by whipping out a pistol and pumping a slug into Mart, whereupon Tom, Merritt, and several others produced weapons and opened fire. The narrow room quickly became hazy with acrid white smoke, but the cattlemen found their targets.

Williams and officer T. M. Daniels slumped to the floor, mortally wounded. Policemen William Cherry and Andrew Melville broke for the door, but Cherry was killed as he stepped outside and Melville was hit as he sprinted away. Melville managed to stagger to the Huling Hotel, where he died four weeks later. The two policemen outside disappeared when the shooting started, and the black officer vaulted onto his mount and galloped toward Austin.

Merritt and Tom carried their wounded brother to their mother's house a block away, then joined their fellow gunmen in heading for the open range. F. L. Britton immediately led a dozen members of the State Police to Lampasas, where he arrested Jerry Scott, the bedridden Mart Horrell, Jim Grizzell, and cowboy Allen Whitecroft. These prisoners were taken to Austin, then transferred to the jail in Georgetown, twenty-five miles north of Austin. Mart's wife Artemisa, who was Jim Grizzell's sister, was permitted to nurse the wounded man in his cell.

The Horrells determined to rescue their incarcerated comrades. When Artemisa Horrell finally sent word that Mart had recovered sufficiently to travel, on Friday night, May 2, the four Horrell brothers sallied into Georgetown at the head of a large party of armed men and rode boldly to the jail. While the others stood guard with rifles, Bill Bowen dismounted and assaulted the door with a sledgehammer.

Aroused townspeople rushed toward the jail and both parties began firing. Bowen ignored a bullet which drew blood and kept swinging until the door shattered. When A. S. Fisher, a local lawyer, was shot in the leg and side, the citizens retreated and the Horrell party thundered triumphantly out of town.[9]

The wanted men remained at large in Lampasas County. Although there now seemed to be scant enthusiasm for trying to arrest these lethal desperadoes, the Horrell brothers decided to move west out of Texas jurisdiction. Livestock was rounded up, wagons were packed, and other preparations were made for the exodus from Lampasas County. The Horrell clan, including Bill Bowen and Ben Turner, along with several other cowboy-gunmen, comprised such a formidable force that they went unchallenged by authorities. The Horrells even informed Sheriff S. T. Denson of their exit route, audaciously confident that they would not be molested. In Coleman County they halted long enough to transact a cattle deal. Unhurriedly the Horrells led their party into New Mexico Territory, settling their herd for the winter on leased range near the head of the Hondo River in vast, lawless Lincoln County.

The younger Horrell, Ben, continued the family custom of drunkenly shooting up the nearest town. Ben and a few friends were thus employed in tiny Lincoln on the night of December 1, 1873, when a constable threatened arrest. A shootout erupted, resulting in the death of the constable, Ben, and two of his drinking companions. The Texans on the Hondo River, of course, vowed revenge. Within days two area Mexicans were killed on Horrell range. The Horrells fought off a posse, then raided a Mexican wedding dance at a residence in Lincoln, shooting through windows and doors and killing four men.

Rewards were posted for the Horrells, but a deputy sheriff was hauled out of his bed and shot to death. During the "Horrell War"[10] there were more than thirty casualties, a violent preview of the Lincoln County War that would gain notoriety for Billy the Kid a few years later. In addition to Ben Horrell, brother-in-law Ben Turner was slain, and with the countryside mobilizing against them, the Texans suddenly ended the Horrell War by pulling out in February 1874. As they headed back to Texas, there was an all-out gun battle at Hueco Tanks. Two Horrell gunmen were mortally wounded, but the Texans killed five opponents, and the decimated pursuit posse limped back to New Mexico. They would experience trouble with Apaches there, but by early March the Horrells were back in the Lampasas area.

News of the violent trek from New Mexico to Texas preceded their return. Albertus Sweet, recently elected sheriff of Lampasas County, led a search for the fugitives spearheaded by a new twenty-man company of minutemen. On March 6 a

The Horrell Brothers

Bill ....b. 1838 ...... Died in Civil War
John .... b. 1841 ...... Shot dead in 1868
Sam ..... b. 1843 ...... Died in bed in 1930!
Mart .... b. 1846 ...... Lynched in 1878
Tom ..... b. 1850 ...... Lynched in 1878
Ben ..... b. 1851 ...... Killed in 1873 gunfight
Merritt ... b. 1853 ...... Killed by Pink in 1877

large posse jumped part of the Horrell gang, wounding Jerry Scott and another partisan and capturing a third man. Merritt Horrell also was nicked, but he escaped, along with Mart and Tom, who rode up during the fight, then spurred away under fire into the brush.

But the minutemen never followed up this foray. The departure of the Union occupation army led to the resounding defeat of Governor E. J. Davis by Democrat Richard Coke in the election of 1873. With Texans back in control of their state, the despised State Police force was dissolved and, in 1874, Maj. John B. Jones organized the Frontier Battalion of Texas Rangers. The Horrell brothers, hiding out in the countryside, were advised "by the best citizens of Lampasas County" that the time was favorable to clear up the charges relating to the slaying of four State Policemen. The trial was not held until October 1876, and a sympathetic jury acquitted Mart, Merritt, and Tom without leaving the jury box.[11]

Mart, Merritt, Tom, and Sam, along with their families, lived in comparative tranquility during the latter part of the 1870s, trying to rebuild their cattle herd on a spread about ten miles southeast of Lampasas on Mesquite Creek in Burnet County. Their father had been slain by Apaches, Ben and John had been killed in New Mexico gunfights, and Bill had died during the Civil War. Apparently the surviving brothers were trying to raise their families in peace. But the Horrells continued to drink in Lampasas saloons, and their primary method of rebuilding their herds appeared to be rustling. After gunning down State Policemen, engineering a daring jailbreak, defying lawmen, battling posses and Apache warriors, and even receiving not guilty verdicts from the local legal system, the remaining Horrells seemed to feel that the lawless frontier conditions they had experienced throughout their lifetimes would continue indefinitely. However, when the Horrells turned their rustling proclivities against Pink Higgins, they would arouse an adversary who used his guns with just as much ruthlessness and deadly skill as they did.

4

The Horrell-Higgins Feud

"Mr. Horrell, this is to settle some cow business."

Pink to Merritt Horrell just before shooting him

LAMPASAS COUNTY WAS RIPE for a blood feud in the 1870s. For nearly two decades settlers had defended themselves against Comanche raiders. Saloon fights were commonplace, and rustling added to the general air of lawlessness.

The most spectacular shootout was the 1873 battle in Jerry Scott's saloon in which Mart Horrell was wounded and four State Policemen were slain. But there was plenty of other lethal gunplay, as described by Lampasas historian Jeffrey Jackson.[1] In August 1875, for example, Charles Keith murdered William Britnal. Sentenced to two years in prison, Keith was placed in the Burnet County jail, but in December 1876 he escaped along with two other prisoners—including Horrell brother-in-law Bill Bowen. In November 1875 Deputy Sheriff W. S. Douglass attempted to take into custody for questioning a local dentist, Dr. J. W. Hudson. But Hudson drew a pistol, and in the ensuing flurry of shots Douglass inflicted fatal wounds with his Winchester. In 1876 Mark Short was arrested in another county and brought to Lampasas to stand trial for the 1873 assault of Sheriff S. T. Denson. (There is no existing record of the trial.) In September the former sheriff's son, Sam Denson, found Short in a saloon.

"Mark Short," announced Denson, "you are my meat!" Denson killed his father's attacker with three shots, then escaped on horseback. He rode to Montana and changed his name, but he would return to Lampasas in 1892 and win a not guilty verdict from a friendly jury.

In the same month as the Short killing, September 1876, County Attorney B. F. Hamilton was called an "S.O.B." by Newton Cook. Hamilton confronted Cook in front of a Lampasas saloon. Producing a derringer, Hamilton managed only to shoot himself in the hand. Cook angrily pulled a pistol and triggered a shot at Hamilton, who fled to the live oak trees around the town square. Constable Elwood Bean, brandishing his own gun, pursued Hamilton.

Tom and Merritt Horrell, acting in the unfamiliar role of peacemakers, averted bloodshed by disarming Hamilton and Bean, respectively. Within a few months, however, the Horrells would again become involved in gunplay, and a great deal of blood would be shed—including some of their own.

Rustling remained a widespread problem on the open ranges of Lampasas County, and the Horrell brothers, with their casual attitude toward the law, were regarded as ready practitioners of this commonplace but dangerous activity of the cattle frontier. The Horrells even stole horses from "an old pioneer preacher," L. R. Milligan. Not one to turn the other cheek, "the preacher took a gun in his pocket, went down to the Horrells, and took [his horse] back."[2]

Feuding in Texas

The unusually violent past of Texas created an atmosphere which animated feudists. For more than a century Spaniards, Mexicans, Anglo settlers, Texas Rangers, and the U.S. Army fought Comanches and Kiowas. Texans engaged in legendary battles at the Alamo, San Jacinto, and Sabine Pass. The Reconstruction period produced lynching and an explosion of gunfighting. A survey of 255 Western gunfights and 589 shootouts reveals that more gunfights—nearly 160—occurred in Texas than in any other Western state or territory.

The first Texas feud was the largest in scale. East Texas' Regulator-Moderator War during the 1840s squared off more than 150 men per side in two factions which defied the peacemaking efforts of the Republic government of President Sam Houston. The bloody Sutton-Taylor feud lasted from 1867 through 1875 and involved the murderous John Wesley Hardin on the side of the Taylors. The Lee-Peacock feud caused bloodshed from 1867 until 1871. The Mason County War was a violent event of 1875. A decade and a half later, Richmond was rocked by bloodletting between the Jaybirds and the Woodpeckers. At the turn of the century East Texas was the scene of the Broocks-Wall feud.

Many Texas feudists had roots from the Ozarks to other mountainous areas where feuding traditions were strong. Such immigrants tended to settle in familiar environments, such as the hills of East Texas or the low mountains of Central Texas, where a great deal of Texas feuding would take place. The Horrell family moved from Arkansas to the Hill Country of Lampasas County; the brothers displayed the clannishness and troublemaking propensities of feudists, and when they crossed Pink Higgins, another bloody Texas vendetta erupted.

In May 1876, Merritt Horrell stole a yearling from the range of Pink Higgins and sold the animal to his brother-in-law, Jim Grizzell, who owned a meat market in Lampasas. On Monday, May 12, Pink rode into town and saw his yearling tied to one of the live oak trees around the square. Pink immediately retrieved his property and swore out a warrant for Horrell's arrest. In court it was proven that the yearling was Pink's property "and that Horrell had no claim whatsoever to the animal, but the jury, for reasons perfectly satisfactory to itself, rendered a verdict of 'not guilty.'" Disgusted over this failure of the legal system, Pink grimly warned Merritt "that he would never bother the law with him again, but he would settle the matter himself with a Winchester rifle."[3]

Merritt underestimated the deadly seriousness of Pink's threat. Perhaps the Horrells' legal exoneration in October 1876 added to Merritt's arrogance. On Saturday, January 20, 1877, a cold and drizzly winter day, Merritt drove a small herd into Lampasas to settle a debt to cattle dealer Alex Northington. Several of the bunch belonged to Pink Higgins, and Northington prudently notified him. Pink quickly rode into town and cut out his cattle, leaving word that if Merritt wanted the livestock back they would be held in a local pen overnight.

Merritt was wise enough to stay away from the cattle pen, but Pink grimly decided it was time to take action. On Monday, accompanied by Bob Mitchell and Sam Hess, Pink rode into town looking for Merritt. Winchester at the ready, Pink walked into Merritt's favorite haunt, the saloon where the 1873 shootout with the State Police had exploded. Merritt was standing beside the stove at the rear of the room, warming himself.

"Mr. Horrell," announced Pink, "this is to settle some cow business."[4]

Pink triggered a Winchester round into Horrell. The impact knocked Merritt off his feet, but he rose shakily and leaned on the shoulder of a man named Ervin. Pink fired again, and once more Merritt was slammed to the floor. (Ervin must have been relieved that Pink was an accurate marksman.) Pink cold-bloodedly triggered two more bullets into Merritt, who died almost instantly.[5]

Pink and his men rode east of town toward the Horrell ranch on Mesquite Creek, apparently searching for more prey. Tom Horrell was riding unarmed toward town when Merritt's friends galloped up with news of the shooting. Tom headed back toward the ranch to warn Mart, but he was intercepted by the Higgins party, now half a dozen strong.

Some of Pink's men wanted to kill Tom. "It will be just another Horrell less," explained one hard-bitten partisan with deadly logic, "and we had better kill him now as we will have to sooner or later."[6]

"No, by God," insisted Bob Mitchell, "you can't kill an unarmed man."[7]

Aware that he was going to need allies, Pink reluctantly gave in to his brother-in-law, who was strongly built "and a

Looking west on the Lampasas square, site of the 1877 battle between the Horrell and Higgins factions. The second building to the left, obscured by an oak tree, housed Jerry Scott's Saloon, where the Horrells shot it out with State Policemen in 1873 and where Pink killed Merritt Horrell in 1877.
(Photo by Standard Studio, Lampasas)

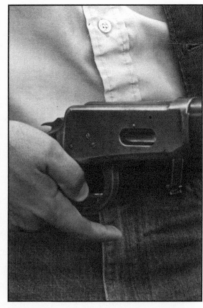

Throughout his long career as a rancher-gunman, Pink Higgins' favorite weapon was a Winchester. When he used it rapid-fire at close quarters, he would slam the lever back and trip the trigger with his thumb, gaining a fraction of a second. He probably used this unorthodox technique when he killed Merritt Horrell.

(Photo courtesy Ted Leach)

terrific fighter." Another brother-in-law, Bill Wren, was even larger, "ham-handed" and 6'3. Ben and Tom Terry were married to Pink's sisters and also would provide needed support, along with a number of friends. "Some men probably said hard things about the Horrells and then were forced to take up with the Mitchells [and Pink] to protect themselves, and it was the same way on the other side," explained John Nichols, regarding the growth of the feud. "Men got into talking and then had to take sides."[8]

Pink would need all the help he could find. Sheriff Sweet asked for assistance from the Texas Rangers, and sixteen men were sent from Company C, headquartered in Llano to the southwest. The Rangers, aided by a posse which included Mart and Tom Horrell, arrested Higgins partisans Nat Arnold,

Winchester '73

It is not known what kind of weapons John Higgins provided his son Pink during the 1860s. When Pink rode after Comanches, surely he was armed with a cap-and-ball revolver in case of a close-quarter fight on horseback. But in 1873 the Colt .45 Peacemaker was introduced, and by 1877, when the Horrell-Higgins feud was at its height, it is likely that Pink's cap-and-ball handgun had been replaced by this classic cartridge revolver.

Pink always preferred a rifle to a pistol, however, and like many Westerners his weapon of choice was a Winchester. Perhaps Pink earlier had used a Henry repeater, introduced in 1860 as the first practical lever-action rifle. The first Winchester, a lever-action repeater with a loading port on the side of the receiver, was introduced in 1866, and Pink may have used this model. Then Winchester produced the Model 1873, which utilized a .44-caliber center fire cartridge. An immediate classic, the Winchester '73 became the best-selling rifle in the West, so popular that in 1878 Colt chambered its single-action Peacemaker for the same .44 cartridge so that a man could use interchangeable ammunition in his revolver and his shoulder gun.

Pink became a noted marksman with his Winchester, and used it instead of a revolver at close range by tripping the trigger with his thumb while working the lever rapid-fire. Pink armed his men with the Model 1873 during the Horrell-Higgins feud. Later he switched to a .30-30, probably a Model 1894, the first lever-action repeater designed for smokeless cartridges and the first Winchester to pass the one million mark in sales. Of course, when using any model, Pink Higgins was deadly accurate with a Winchester.

Maybelline Lovejoy, Bill Tinker, and George Ware on charges of complicity in the murder of Merritt Horrell. Lovejoy was released for lack of evidence, Arnold and Ware posted bond, and Tinker, who could not raise bail, was jailed; later he provided an acceptable alibi. Pink remained at large, perhaps because law officers did not conduct much of a search for the killer of a rustler and troublemaker. C. L. Sonnichsen interviewed elderly Lampasans in 1944, sixty-seven years after the feud. "The old timers say now that Pink never left the county and did pretty much as he pleased," Sonnichsen wrote, "staying most of the time at the home of one of his friends."[9]

While Pink remained at large, the Horrells maintained a low profile for the next two months. Sobered by the violent death of another brother, the surviving Horrells refrained from retaliation—and again Pink seized the initiative. Having opened the bloodletting by killing cattle thief Merritt Horrell, Pink aggressively decided once more to carry the fight to the Horrells.

On Monday, March 26, Tom and Mart were scheduled for an appearance in district court before Judge W. A. Blackburn. A detail of Texas Rangers rode into town in case of trouble. Their anticipation of violence proved accurate, but Pink outguessed the Rangers—and the Horrells—regarding location.

Pink, Bill Wren, Bill Tinker, and a couple of other men set an ambush five miles east of Lampasas at a stream afterward christened "Battle Branch." When Tom and Mart reached the creek about ten in the morning, they stopped to water their mounts. Without warning, the hidden gunmen opened fire.

Tom was knocked out of the saddle by a bullet in the hip, and Mart suffered a flesh wound in the neck. His horse bolted, but Mart controlled the animal and turned back to his immobile brother. Brandishing his Winchester, Mart jumped off his skittish mount and, consumed with battle lust, routed the ambushers with a one-man charge. Mart managed to carry Tom to the nearby house of John Tinnin, then galloped into town for help.[10]

Pink and his men rode northwest for five miles, then three members of the party split off to the northwest. The Rangers

Battle Branch, a few miles east of Lampasas, where Tom and Mart Horrell fought their way past a Higgins ambush on March 26, 1877.

(Photo by Karon O'Neal)

came out to investigate, and followed the trail without over-taking any suspects. Bill Tinker soon was taken into custody, but again he provided an alibi and was released. Hoping for the same results, Bill Wren decided to turn himself in on Monday, April 2, a week after the ambush. Apparently Wren, too, was discharged from custody.

Three weeks later, and three months to the day after the death of Merritt Horrell—on April 22, 1877—Pink and Bob Mitchell surrendered to the Rangers. The continuing presence of the Rangers probably dissuaded other shootouts between the feudists. Pink and Bob Mitchell, who surely had no inten-tion of being confined inside the crackerbox Lampasas jail, were held in the Ranger camp. Soon they each were granted a $10,000 bond, and after posting surety, Pink and Mitchell again were on the loose.[11]

Although all principals were free from custody, an uneasy truce prevailed for the next few weeks, and summer campers began to arrive at Lampasas to take the waters. Then on Thursday, May 31, "detachments of the two factions" encountered each other on School Creek, north of Lampasas near the Higgins-Mitchell neighborhood. After a flurry of shots the Horrell riders retreated, "and the Higgins party captured a field glass, a saddle and other plunder from their adversaries."[12]

There were rumors of other violent incidents during the "guerrilla warfare" of Lampasas County. More than three decades later Pink stated that two black men who worked in Lampasas were paid by the Horrells to report on the movement of the Higgins faction. Supposedly, Pink and three of his men played a game of Seven Up to determine who would put these informers "out of the way," after which Pink "got both of them himself."[13] One writer described a siege of the Horrell stronghold by Pink and fourteen of his men. After two days of sniping, ammunition ran low and Pink withdrew, having succeeded only in wounding two Horrell men. This same writer related two separate shootings in which Pink killed Horrell riders Zeke Terrell and Ike Lantier.[14] No other source mentions Terrell or Lantier, however, and there also is no corroboration of the other two deaths, although the disappearance of two black men in 1870s Texas might easily have gone unnoticed.

Feeling that he was constantly being stalked, Pink would not allow a light in his house after dark, and even when "he stepped to the woodpile his Winchester went along." He also said that he engaged a spy, "who posed as a gunman from Mexico, and got into their employ," then tipped off Pink about Horrell movements by placing "unsigned letters in an old hollow tree."[15]

A number of cases regarding the feud were pending in district court in Lampasas. But on Monday, June 4, 1877, the flimsy court building was broken into and all district court records, including cases unrelated to the feud, were stolen. These records presumably were burned; no documents have survived. Richard Hubbard, the 400-pound governor of Texas, posted a $500 reward for the courthouse burglars. Lampasans understood that the culprits were Tom Bowen and three other Horrell partisans, but $500 did not seem to be a sufficient amount to lure anyone into the murderous feud.

Three days after the court records were stolen a bloody confrontation erupted, apparently by accident, in Lampasas on Thursday morning, June 7. Learning of the theft of legal documents, Pink and Bob Mitchell decided to ride into town to reaffirm their bonded status. Although not expecting the Horrells to be in Lampasas, they took the precaution of bringing an armed escort, perhaps as many as a dozen men. Riding

A Grisly Miracle on the Range

An oft-told tale about Pink Higgins involves him patrolling a pasture and sighting one of the steers under his protection being butchered. Pink pulled his Winchester and drew a bead on the thief who had shot the steer. From ninety yards he dropped the rustler with one bullet.

Angrily Pink stuffed the rustler's corpse inside the disemboweled animal, then rode into town to the sheriff's office. He told the astounded law officers where they could ride onto the range and "find a miracle taking place—a cow giving birth to a man!"

One version of this story placed the "miracle" on Pink's Lampasas County range during his trouble with the Horrell brothers. But such noted historians as Walter P. Webb, in The Texas Rangers, and Mari Sandoz, in The Cattlemen, reported the incident on the Spur Ranch while Pink was working as a protection man. The story may be apocryphal, but it is so persistent that it could indeed be based on fact. Certainly it provides an unforgettable part of the gunfighting legend of Pink Higgins.

in from the north along the Hamilton Road, several of the party dropped off about two and a half miles from Lampasas. While Ben and Alonzo Mitchell, Newt Higgins, John Cox, and other riders waited, Pink and Bob Mitchell proceeded on into town, accompanied by Bill Wren and Ben Terry.[16]

Unknown to the Higgins party, a large Horrell faction was in Lampasas. Lounging around the well on the public square were Tom, Mart, and Sam Horrell; their friends included Bob McGee and a hardcase known as Jim Buck Miller (alias Jim Buck Palmer and Buck Waldrop), who had just signed on with the Horrells.

Bill Wren and Bob Mitchell rode beside each other as Pink and Ben Terry trailed a short distance to the rear. At about ten o'clock they passed in front of the Star Hotel a block north of the square, then turned south toward the square on Live Oak Street. Tom Horrell saw his adversaries approaching and shouted out an alarm: "Over yonder comes the Higginses."

Unlimbering their guns, Tom and Sam Horrell headed toward the enemy, taking cover behind a load of wire in front of Mellon's Store, on the northwest corner of the square. Mart and Jim Buck Miller darted across Live Oak Street to Fulton & Townsen's Store in a corner building west of the well. Gunfire suddenly broke out, and Wren and Mitchell hastily dismounted to find cover on opposite sides of Live Oak Street. Wren ducked behind a hackberry tree in the wagon yard adjacent to the Star Hotel, while Mitchell headed for the alley to the west.[17]

Tom Horrell previously had lost the sight in his right eye, but he peered around the corner of the limestone building, hoping to fire at Mitchell, who was behind a picket fence. Mitchell, however, fired first, triggering a round each time Tom's head came into view. Mitchell squeezed off three shots, each time coming so close that the bullet knocked rock dust into Tom's good eye. Tom "would jerk his head back and wipe the dust out before shooting again," according to an eyewitness, while Tom's bullets hit the fence near Bob's head.[18]

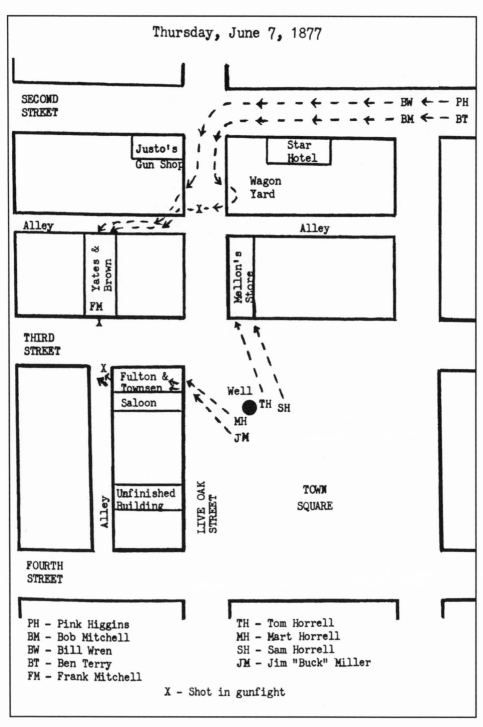

Lampasas—Thursday, June 7, 1877

Although Bill Wren fired a shot or two, he could not find a good target, so with boldness—and foolhardiness—he decided to sprint across the street to join Bob Mitchell. "Get back there or they will get you!" warned Bob.

"I can't see anybody to shoot at," said Bill impatiently.[19]

As soon as Wren emerged into the open he drew fire, and a bullet caught him in the thigh. Wren stumbled on to Mitchell's position, then Bob helped his wounded ally toward a safer place up the alley. They entered the rear of a two-story building which housed the Yates & Brown Store on the lower floor, then they struggled upstairs to the law office of Judge J. A. Abney. Within moments they were joined by Bob's younger brother, Frank Mitchell, who had been unloading flour from a wagon at the Yates & Brown Store when the firing broke out.

During the first flurry of gunfire, Pink and Ben Terry rode behind Juan Escobedo's Gun Shop. Pink quickly decided to bring his nearby reinforcements into the fray. Spurring their mounts, Pink and Ben retraced their path past the Star Hotel, then galloped back up the Hamilton Road toward the men who were waiting a couple of miles away.

On their own for the time being, Bob Mitchell and the wounded Bill Wren at least had been reinforced by Frank Mitchell. "Honest, industrious, and inoffensive,"[20] Frank was a thirty-four-year-old family man who previously had taken no part in the feud. But he and his father were in town on business, and when Frank saw his brother under fire, blood called to blood. Frank was unarmed, but he borrowed a revolver from Bill Wren and went downstairs to find a target. Carefully Frank slipped out the front door of the store to peer down Third Street.

In the meantime, Mart Horrell and Jim Buck Miller went through Fulton & Townsen's Store and passed through the rear door into the alley, perhaps intending to flank their opponents. They were noticed by Frank Mitchell, who fired one shot and drilled Jim Buck Miller in the chest. There was immediate return fire, and Frank was hit with a Winchester slug. Frank staggered back inside, then collapsed behind a store counter and died. Although both Mart and Jim Buck had squeezed off Winchester rounds, "Mart claimed he was the one that shot Mitchell, as he wanted the credit."[21]

Mart helped the badly wounded Jim Buck Miller (who would die the next day) down the alley to an unfinished rock building that faced the square. There they were joined by Tom and Sam Horrell, along with a few other allies. By the time Pink thundered back into town with his reinforcements, the Horrell party had forted up inside the rock structure. "A regiment of men could not have driven them out," declared a newspaper account.[22]

Pink did not have a regiment, and with Frank Mitchell dead and the redoubtable Bill Wren wounded, no one intended to charge the riflemen inside the rock building. The fight became a sniping duel, and community leaders approached both factions with attempts to arrange a truce.

Local businessmen knew that if Lampasas continued to be a battleground, summer tourists would avoid such a dangerous spa. And the feudists realized that the current fight had stabilized into a standoff. About noon Pink and his men rode out of town, while the Horrells submitted to "arrest." When darkness fell the Horrells were released from protective custody, apparently by prearrangement, and allowed to ride to their homes. "Turmoil and excitement prevailed all over the country," recounted the *Lampasas Leader*, "and people were expecting every day to hear of a clash between the warring factions."[23]

Jim Buck Miller died on Tuesday, and the Horrells buried yet another man. Frank Mitchell was interred in the Townsen Cemetery, near his home, a sobering loss for the Higgins-Mitchell faction.

Sheriff Albertus Sweet wrote to Maj. John B. Jones, commander of the Frontier Battalion of Texas Rangers, with another request for help. Major Jones gathered a detail of fifteen Rangers and rode into Lampasas on Monday, June 14, a week after the two-hour shootout in town. The Rangers camped at Hancock Springs and during the next several days were highly active in helping Sheriff Sweet and other area officers to round up fugitives.

None of the arrests were of members of the Horrell or Higgins factions. The Horrell brothers left the county after the shootout in town and did not return for nearly four weeks, while Pink and his allies stayed on good behavior. After the Horrells reentered the county early in July, Major Jones reported that he had begun diplomatic efforts "to intercede and endeavor to reconcile the difficulty and thus terminate this long continued feud. I am on good terms with both parties and hope to effect something towards the desired object in a few days."[24]

But two weeks later the Horrells were the chief suspects in the death of Carson Graham, a Higgins rider. Graham was

Pink Higgins, seated at right, with his crew after driving a herd from Lampasas County up the Chisholm Trail to Kansas. Front row, from left: Felix Castello, Jess Standard, Bob Mitchell, Pink. Back row: Powell Woods, Unknown, Buck Allen, Alonzo Mitchell. **(Courtesy Standard Studio, Lampasas)**

gunned down by unknown parties near Townsen's Mill on Tuesday, July 24. Major Jones was now determined to bring the feud to a halt.

Jones and four men rode north to investigate the killing, but found nothing except rumors about the Horrells. A couple of days later, however, one or more Higgins partisans brought word of the whereabouts of the Horrells. At sunset on Friday, July 27, Bill Wren, Bob Mitchell, or Alonzo Mitchell—or all three—rode into the Ranger camp at Hancock Springs with news that the entire Horrell party was at Mart's ranch southeast of town on Mesquite Creek. Major Jones ordered Sgt. N. O. Reynolds to take seven privates and, guided by Wren and the Mitchell brothers, try to arrest the Horrells while they were asleep.

Reynolds and his party found the Horrell stronghold in the darkness. Eleven men, along with a few women and children, were sleeping inside the house, several on beds in the main room and the others curled up on floor pallets. The Rangers waited until five in the morning before closing in on the ranch house. A heavy rain was falling, and the lawmen tiptoed inside undetected. Each officer leveled a cocked rifle at the slumbering men, then Reynolds awoke the room by telling Mart he was in the custody of Texas Rangers.[25]

The Horrell men bolted upright and for a horrible moment seemed to believe that it was their enemies who were inside the house. Mart mumbled that they could not surrender, and Tom defiantly snarled that they might as well die fighting as submit to mobs in Lampasas. Sam grabbed for his Winchester, but Reynolds scuffled with him. The gun went off, igniting a mattress but quieting the room.

Reynolds capitalized on this opportunity, warning the Horrells of the firepower he commanded and assuring them that his men were indeed Texas Rangers. As the atmosphere became calmer Reynolds pledged his word that he would maintain a Ranger guard over any prisoners until a preliminary hearing could be arranged and bond set.

"Boys, this seems reasonable," said Mart, eyeing the cocked Winchesters as he rose to his feet. "I believe these Rangers can be relied on to protect us. Besides this fight has been thrust on us. If we can get a hearing we can give bond."[26]

Sam, Mart, and Tom finally submitted to custody, after Reynolds agreed to release the other men. Major Jones promptly employed his considerable skills as a negotiator, and within two days produced a conciliatory document signed by the Horrells:

Lampasas Texas
July 30th 1877

Messrs Pink Higgins Robert Mitchell and William Wrenn.
Gentlemen:

From this standpoint, looking back over the past with its terrible experiences both to ourselves and to you, and to the suffering which has been entailed upon both of our families and our friends by the quarrel in which we have been involved with its repeated fatal consequences, and looking to a termination of the same, and a peaceful, honorable and happy adjustment of our difficulties which shall leave both ourselves and you, all our self respect and sense of unimpaired honor, we have determined to take the initiatory in a move for reconciliation. Therefore we present this paper in which we hold ourselves in honor bound to lay down our arms and to end the strife in which we have been engaged against you and exert our utmost efforts to entirely eradicate all enmity from the minds of our friends who have taken sides with us in the feud hereinbefore alluded to.

And we promise furthermore to abstain from insulting or injuring you and your friends, to bury the bitter past forever, and join with you as good citizens in undoing the evil which has resulted from our quarrel, and to leave nothing undone which we can effect to bring about a complete consummation of the purpose to which we have herein committed ourselves.

Provided:

That you shall on your part take upon yourselves a similar obligation as respects our friends and us, and shall address a paper to us with your signatures thereupon, such a paper as this which we freely offer you. Hoping that this may bring about the happy result which it aims at we remain

Yours respectfully,

Thos. L. Horrell

S. W. Horrell

C. O. M. Horrell

Witness

Jno. B. Jones

Maj. Frontier Battalion

The Horrell brothers, who had almost no education, could not have written such a letter. This document, and the one which followed, almost certainly came from the pen of Major Jones. The forty-two-year-old Jones was a native of South Carolina; he had enjoyed a fine formal education and had risen to the rank of major during the Civil War. Steeped in the traditions of the South, Jones understood the art of negotiating a peaceful solution between potential duelists. Dueling was commonplace in the South, but once a challenge was issued, friends and "seconds" of the antagonists made every effort to arrive at some sort of apology or retraction that would satisfy honor short of conducting the proposed duel. Carefully worded notes and letters often averted violence, and Jones clearly was a master of the peacemaker's language.

On Tuesday, July 31, the day after the Horrells signed their letter of conciliation, Major Jones arrested Pink Higgins, Bob Mitchell, and Bill Wren. They quickly posted bond and were released, but Jones showed them the Horrell letter, emphasizing that the brothers had initiated a pledge "to abstain from insulting or injuring you and your friends, to bury the bitter past forever. . . ." Now the honor of the Higgins faction demanded "a similar obligation."

The following day, August 1, while Major Jones crafted a suitable response, the Horrell brothers were released after posting bond. Mart tearfully wrung the hand of Sergeant Reynolds and announced, "You are undoubtedly the bravest man in the world today."[27]

On Thursday, the day after the Horrells were released, Pink, Bob Mitchell, and Bill Wren signed a letter of reply. Pink had no more education than the Horrells, and the language is the same as in the first document. Thus Jones had artfully answered his own letter:[28]

> Lampasas Texas
> Aug 2nd 1877

Mess. Mart. Tom and Sam Horrell
Gentlemen

Your favor dated the 30th ult. was handed to us by Maj. Jones. We have carefully noted its contents and approve most sincerely the spirit of the communication. It would be difficult for us to express in words the mental disturbance to ourselves which the sad quarrel with its fatal consequences, alluded to in your letter occasioned. And now with passions cooled we look back with you sorrowfully to the past, and promise with you to commence at once and instantly the task of repairing the injuries resulting from the difficulty as far as our power extends to do.

Certainly we will make every effort to restore good feeling with those who armed themselves in our quarrel, and on our part we lay down our weapons with the honest purpose to regard the feud which has existed between you and us as a by gone thing to be remembered only to bewail.

Furthermore as you say we will abstain from offering insult or injury to you or yours and will seek to bring all our friends to a complete conformity with the agreements herein expressed by us.

As we hope for future peace and happiness for ourselves and for those who look to us for guidance and protection and as we desire to take position as good law-abiding citizens and preservers of peace and order we subscribe ourselves.

> Respectfully & C.
> J. P. Higgins
> R. A. Mitchell
> W. R. Wren

Witness
Jno. B. Jones
Maj. Frontier Battalion

A week passed with no further trouble, and on August 9 the *Lampasas Dispatch* proclaimed in headlines:

PEACE RESTORED IN LAMPASAS!
THE HIGGINS AND HORRELL PARTIES
HAVE LAID DOWN THEIR ARMS!!

The month after peace was declared, on September 17, 1877, Malinda Caledonia Higgins was born to Betty and Pink. Little Cullen Higgins, not yet two, now had a baby sister. With the end of the feud, Pink now was free to devote himself to family life and to the cattle business.

But even though both factions lived up to their oaths and did not resume fighting, the atmosphere remained tense. Peace prevailed primarily because the Texas Rangers maintained a detachment in Lampasas. Although Pink would engage in no further shootouts with the Horrell brothers, the twenty-six-year-old Texan now commanded widespread respect as a gunman. The events of 1877 earned Pink the reputation of a deadly shootist, and his temperament and activities would continue to add to that lethal reputation. After the Horrell-Higgins feud, life would never return to normal for Pink. Perhaps, for this tough and courageous son of the frontier, violent confrontations would be an inevitable part of his life.

5

Aftermath of a Range War

"Mosty, don't make a motion or I will kill you."

Pink to a man who refused to pay off a debt

FOLLOWING THE HORRELL-HIGGINS BLOODLETTING of 1877, rustlers prudently avoided the ranges of Lampasas County. Pink continued to take personal precautions, however, and there were occasional tense moments. In March 1878, for example, court hearings related to the feud were held in Lampasas. The former combatants rode into town armed to the teeth, but a squad of Texas Rangers was on the scene to preserve the peace.

If peace prevailed in Lampasas County, the Horrells soon found trouble elsewhere. On May 28, 1878, a Bosque County storekeeper named J. F. Vaughn was murdered by a gang of horsemen who stole $3,000 from his safe. As the riders galloped into the night, witnesses sent a volley of gunfire after them, and a horse was wounded. Capt. W. H. Glenn, a detective from Waco, followed the getaway trail south to Mart Horrell's ranch and discovered that the wounded animal belonged to Bill Crabtree. Crabtree had ridden and fought alongside the Horrells for years.

On August 24, 1878, Glenn showed up in Meridian, the seat of Bosque County, with the twenty-five-year-old gunman in custody. Crabtree implicated Mart and Tom Horrell in Vaughn's death and on September 8 the two brothers were arrested and taken to Meridian for a hearing.

During the two-week proceedings Crabtree turned state's evidence against Mart and Tom, and the presiding judge, an official named Childress, ordered the Horrells jailed without bail. Crabtree immediately left town, but just as he reached the outskirts of Meridian an unknown assailant shot him from the saddle and left him to die under a tree.

In October Judge W. A. Blackburn requested that Mart and Tom Horrell be returned to Lampasas to answer charges relating to the feud, but Judge Childress declined to release them, commenting that feelings were so strong in Meridian that it would be unsafe for them outside the stone jail. It also proved unsafe for them inside the jail.

About eight-thirty Sunday evening, December 15, 1878, a mob of more than one hundred masked men converged on the jail in Meridian. The sheriff already had been lured away by a message that his mother was dying in another town, and the vigilantes gained entry to the building when one of their members announced that he was "Deputy Whitworth." Inside, the two jailers refused to unlock the door to the cell block until the mob threatened to burn the jail with kerosene.

Nearly fifty men crowded toward the Horrell cell, forcing another inmate to hold the light while they opened fire. Tom cowered and vainly tried to elude the bullets, but Mart exhibited the mettle that had propelled him singlehandedly against the bushwhackers at Battle Branch. He viciously rattled the cell door and cursed the vigilantes, and continued the bitter tirade even after he had taken several bullets. A final volley finished the job, and Tom and Mart Horrell died in a pool of blood on the cell floor. It is not improbable to imagine Bob Mitchell, whose brother Frank had been killed by Mart, and Pink as members of the lynch mob.

After the lynching, Judge Blackburn dismissed all charges pertaining to the Horrell-Higgins feud. With all of his brothers dead, Sam Horrell decided not to make it unanimous. He left the state within a few years, moved to California, and died peacefully at the age of ninety-nine in 1936.[1]

Pink Higgins certainly felt no remorse over the bloody demise of Mart and Tom Horrell. For Pink the death of any enemy was good riddance, and he must have believed that Mart and Tom had received their just deserts. Indeed, it was

After Tom and Mart Horrell were lynched in Meridian in 1878, they were buried together in the north part of the Oak Hill Cemetery in Lampasas.

(Photo by Karon O'Neal)

not long before more harsh justice was meted out to surviving members of the Horrell faction.

On the night of April 3, 1879, about a dozen riders arrived at the home of James Collier, who lived eight miles east of Lampasas on Mesquite Creek, near the ranch of Mart Horrell. Collier, who had been a friend of Mart, agreed to leave his wife and go with the riders. The next day he was found hanging from a tree. Pinned to his clothing was a note written by someone with only a rudimentary education:

> FAIR WARNING—EVERY HARBERER—
> THAT HARBERS—THEAVES AND MURDURES—
> WILL BE SERVED—THE SAME—WAY.[2]

Four nights later, on April 7, a group of riders approached the camp of Bill, Thomas, and Jesse Vanwinkle on Little Lucy Creek, north of Lampasas. One of the men claimed to be the sheriff and ordered Bill Vanwinkle to come with them. Thomas and Jesse Vanwinkle stayed in camp, and half an hour or so later, they heard gunfire. The next day they found Bill's bullet-riddled body.

On the night of July 28, 1879, four riders approached the house of Alex Campbell, located on Simms Creek not far from Higgins Gap. Campbell was the stepfather of Gus and William Kinchelo, whose mother was Sam Horrell's sister-in-law. Gus and William were suspected rustlers, and when the night riders asked them to come outside, the brothers made a dash for safety. William was shot to death in the yard. Gus was hit in the wrist, but he managed to escape into the darkness.

None of the night riders were ever identified, and no charges were filed in any of these three killings. Because the victims could be connected with rustling or with the Horrells or both, it might have been easy to speculate that the night riders were members of the Higgins faction. But such speculation also might have been unsafe, and no accusations were made public.

With his most dangerous enemies dead or gone from

Lampasas County, Pink was free to resume his normal activities as a rancher and trail driver. During the early 1880s Pink was in business with a cattleman named Al Shanklin, who was backed by his family. In 1881 Higgins and Shanklin sent 10,000 head of cattle in five herds to Colorado. Bob Fudge was a strapping cowboy who rode with the last of the 1881 herds, and he reminisced that his crew consisted of eight cowboys, a horse wrangler, and a cook. This crew departed in May and delivered their herd to Hugo, Colorado, in August. According to Fudge, Pink and his partner went broke on the 10,000 cattle they contracted for that year, but "Shanklin's people were very wealthy and staked him again." Fudge hired on with Higgins and Shanklin again in 1884, helping to drive 2,500 cows and calves to Charles Goodnight in the Texas Panhandle.[3]

As a stockman Pink was away from home a great deal, buying or selling or delivering animals, trading cattle and horses, hiring drovers, rounding up herds, and leading drives that lasted for months. During one drive, a rider lumbered into camp on a spent horse. He told Pink that he had caught a crooked gambler attempting "to put away an ace in a poker game and had shot and killed him." But now the stranger was being pursued by a gang of vengeful gamblers. Trusting his instincts, Pink gave the stranger a fresh horse and fifty dollars, and the man galloped away to safety.

Years later, Pink traveled to Muskogee, Oklahoma, representing a Texas cattle company in a large livestock transaction. While standing on a main thoroughfare, the tall cattleman was noticed by a citizen, who turned and walked past Pink, then passed again. Pink recognized the beleaguered stranger from the long-ago cattle camp.

"Yes," announced Pink, "it's me."

The citizen wrung Pink's hand in delayed gratitude. Pink learned that his aid to a stranger had helped the man to become a successful and prominent citizen.[4]

Although railroads probed into Texas during the 1870s

and reached West Texas by the 1880s, many cattlemen continued long drives until the mid-1880s. High railroad rates made trail drives to Kansas economical, until the trails were blocked by fences. As late as 1882 Pink took a herd up the old Western Trail to Dodge City. Pink advertised in the *Lampasas Leader* that he wanted to purchase 1,500 head of one- and two-year-olds "for which the highest market prices will be paid." Pink found plenty of cattle; on Tuesday, April 11, he headed north with 1,600 head.[5]

Pink's frequent absences from home contributed to serious stress on his marriage to Betty. On the second day of 1880 the couple's third child, John Thomas Higgins, was born. But within the next year or so Betty entered into an adulterous affair with Dunk Harris, who moved with his parents and brothers in 1881 to Lampasas, where he worked in the

Cool Hand Pink

A Lampasas man proclaimed that he could beat anyone in a chicken liver eating contest. Never one to duck a challenge, Pink Higgins picked up this somewhat unusual gauntlet. Betting was heavy, and the stakes were held by former outlaw Frank James. (After winning release from legal custody in 1885, James lived in numerous places, including Texas. He was in demand as a race starter at county and state fairs, so the chicken liver eating contest may have been part of a Lampasas County Fair.)

It was a real life episode which may have provided inspiration for a classic scene from the 1967 movie *Cool Hand Luke*, in which the title character, played by Paul Newman, wins a wager by eating fifty eggs. In Lampasas, Pink awed onlookers by downing forty-eight chicken livers, while his opponent could manage merely twenty-eight. Since Pink could have stopped at twenty-nine, it may be assumed that he was unusually partial to chicken livers.

family mercantile business. A woman who lived on a ranch in a rural county could not long conceal an illicit romance. When Pink found out, he packed Betty and her personal belongings into a buggy, permitting her to take only Ida May, the daughter from her first marriage, and she left Higgins Gap.[6]

Somewhat surprisingly, Pink did not shoot Dunk Harris, who moved to Goldthwaite a few years later. Perhaps thinking of his three small children, Pink avoided the legal difficulties that a killing would have created. Perhaps, too, Pink occasionally had strayed from wedding vows at the end of trail drives in Dodge City or some other cattle town.

Pink initiated divorce proceedings and agreed to pay the modest legal costs. The divorce was finalized on May 24, 1882,[7] while Pink was on the trail drive to Dodge City. Six-year-old Cullen, four-year-old Malinda, and two-year-old Tom stayed at home with their grandparents, John and Hester Higgins. John and Hester played a significant role in raising the children while Pink was gone.

Partly because he so often was an absentee father, Pink recognized that his children needed a stepmother. He soon found a new wife in pretty Lena Rivers Sweet, daughter of Albertus Sweet, a Confederate veteran who was the sheriff of Lampasas County from 1874 to 1878. In 1881, while serving as deputy marshal of Belton, Sweet was fatally wounded during an attempted arrest. Only thirty-eight when he died, Sweet was brought back to Lampasas for burial. Born on February 9, 1868, Lena was only thirteen when her father was killed; her mother, Lavina, was thirty-two.[8]

Pink and Lena married on June 8, 1883. He was thirty-two and she was fifteen, but her mother had been only thirteen when she married eighteen-year-old Albertus Sweet. Pink towered over his pretty, blue-eyed bride, who brought a sweet and loving temperament to the marriage. Not surprisingly, Lena was deferential to her older husband, and she earned the devotion of her stepchildren.

Lena and Pink had six children of their own, five girls and

Lena Rivers Sweet married Pink Higgins in 1883, when she was fifteen.

(Courtesy Betty L. Giddens)

Believed to be the wedding photo of Pink and Lena, Friday, June 8, 1883.

(Courtesy Betty L. Giddens)

Pink and Lena's first child, Rocky Rivers Higgins, born in 1886.

(Courtesy Betty L. Giddens)

Pink and Lena's first two daughters, Rocky Rivers and Ruby Lake. The next child was dubbed Bonnie Bay, but then the nautical names stopped. **(Courtesy Betty L. Giddens)**

a boy. Their first child was born in 1886 and, taking a cue from Lena's middle name, the parents dubbed their baby Rocky Rivers Higgins. Their next little girl was named Ruby Lake Higgins, and their third daughter was christened Bonnie Bay Higgins. These nautical names ended with their only son, Roy, who suffered from epilepsy. The next daughter, Lorena ("Rena"), was born crippled, and the last child was named Nell.

With trail driving on the decline, Pink opened a meat market in Lampasas as a complement to his cattle business. He also operated a saloon in the same building. But Pink let his customers rely on credit, and when his building burned, he was owed about $3,000. Although Pink had kept no accurate records, he estimated that the debts were evenly split between whiskey accounts and meat bills. "Considerably more than half of the liquor debts were voluntarily paid," reminisced Pink, adding "that if a single one of the meat accounts ever was settled he didn't remember it."[9]

One debt was rather roughly settled by Pink himself. Pink held a note for $100 from L. A. Mosty. Apparently expecting to encounter Mosty in town, Pink carried the note into Lampasas on Wednesday, December 6, 1882. Pink spotted Mosty standing with a few other men in front of C. H. Ross' store. Walking up to Mosty, Pink thrust the note into his hand.

"There is your note," announced Pink firmly. "I have paid and you must pay me."

Mosty threw the note down and tried to retreat into the store. Pink was not wearing a gunbelt or carrying his Winchester, but he had jammed a revolver into a hip pocket, and quickly he gripped the sixgun.

"Mosty, don't make a motion or I will kill you," warned Pink. Then he repeated ominously, "You have got it to pay."

"Hold up," said Mosty, raising his hands. "Hand it here— if it is properly endorsed I will pay it."

"You threw it down," growled Pink, "come out and pick it up."

Mosty walked back outside, picked up the note, and

examined it. "By God," said Mosty, realizing he was cornered, "I want to inform you I have got the money."

Producing a wallet, Mosty counted out ten ten-dollar bills. "You have got your money." Mosty stepped back into the store and muttered, "I am robbed."

Mosty filed a complaint, and in May 1883 a grand jury indicted Pink for aggravated assault. More than a year later, on June 13, 1884, Pink was charged in district court with robbery of $100 by "unlawfully, willfully and feloniously" making an assault upon Mosty.

Pink pled not guilty, and the case came to trial in December 1884. After hearing the witnesses and arguments, Judge W. A. Blackburn presented a lengthy charge to the jury. Judge Blackburn expounded upon the definition of robbery: "If any person by assault, or by violence and *putting the fear of life or bodily injury* [author's italics], shall fraudulently take from the person or possession of another any property, with intent to appropriate the same to his own use, he will be deemed guilty of robbery." Such an offense would demand "confinement in the penitentiary not less than two nor more than ten years."

But Judge Blackburn then added significantly: "While no man has any legal right to collect a debt due him by assault or by violence, and putting in fear of life or bodily injury, yet it does not necessarily follow that a collection thus made is robbery, but might be some other offense. . . ." The judge pointed out that "an

The Lampasas County Courthouse, built in 1883.

(Courtesy Standard Studio, Lampasas)

assault becomes aggravated when committed with deadly weapons under circumstances not amounting to an intent to murder or maim." Aggravated assault would demand a fine of $25 to $1,000, or confinement in the county jail from one month to two years.[10]

The jury declared Pink guilty of aggravated assault, and assessed his punishment as a fine of $100. There was certainly an element of fairness in this decision, but Pink could recall a time when he probably would not even have been brought to court over such an incident.

Despite this pointed indication that law and order was gripping the frontier, Pink never lost his readiness to resort to violence. The purchase of a horse herd across the border from Del Rio led to what Pink regarded as his "hardest fight." Pink's account of this gun battle is the only source of information. Not even the year is known; Pink related that the Texas governor at the time was John Ireland, who served from January 1883 until January 1887. Del Rio during the 1880s was a raw border town. There were only fifty residents in 1880, but the population began to grow after Del Rio became the seat of newly organized Val Verde County in 1885. Records were sketchy, and there were no newspapers. The border was turbulent during this period, and Pink's "hardest fight" might have been shrugged off by locals as just another shootout on the Mexican side of the Rio Grande.

Pink reminisced that he had arranged to buy 125 horses in Mexico. For years Pink bought " 'wet' horses—that is, horses that had swum the Rio Grande River. They had been stolen in Old Mexico and were sold to the cattlemen of Texas for cow ponies."[11] Of course, dealing with Mexican horse thieves could easily lead to trouble.

On this occasion, Pink paid one dollar per head as earnest money, and would pay the balance when the horse herd was delivered to Ciudad Acuna, across the Rio Grande from Del Rio. On the appointed date Pink and three men rode through the dusty streets of Del Rio and crossed the International

Bridge. Pink soon found the horse dealers, but with 125 of his dollars already in their pockets they had no intention of completing the deal.

The Horrell-Higgins feud was years in the past, and Pink had not battled Comanches in well over a decade. But violent response to injury or threats or affronts was never far beneath the surface of Pink Higgins. Pink reminded the Mexicans that they had taken $125 from him as the down payment for a horse herd. He was infuriated when they laughed at him. Feeling safe on his side of the border, one Mexican arrogantly told Pink that he had never seen him before. Pink grimly replied that he certainly would never see him again, and whipped out his gun. He pumped the Mexican full of holes, then led his men in a dash for the Rio Grande.

The way to the International Bridge was blocked, but as the *norteamericanos* sprinted toward the river a score or more of Mexicans opened fire. One of Pink's men was killed and another was wounded. At the river the unwounded herder jumped into the water, urging Pink to swim across with him. But Pink would not leave his wounded partner, and he threatened to shoot the uninjured man if he did not come out of the water and fight. The wounded man was able to work his gun, and, taking cover at the riverbank, Pink and his two companions kept up a lively fire. Pink later said that bullets "fell all around them like hail," but several Mexicans were hit by return fire.

When darkness descended, the besieged Higgins party buried three sixguns and some of their ammunition, so that they would not be weighted down when swimming the river. They secured the other guns and cartridge belts around their necks, then slipped into the water. The two unwounded men supported their injured comrade between them, and swam undetected back to the north bank of the Rio Grande. Pink later declared "that he fought harder then and under less favorable circumstances than ever before or since."[12]

Another livestock deal involving horses again plunged Pink into trouble, this time with the legal system rather than gunplay. While trading horses for cattle through an agent, Pink came in possession of a "wild stag" (hair had grown over the brand). When Pink tried to sell this beast to a meat market in Lampasas, rancher Sam Jennings revealed the overgrown brand and stated that the animal had been stolen from his spread, which was north of Higgins Gap.[13]

Charged with cattle theft, Pink pled not guilty. But the jury was not favorably inclined toward this forty-year-old relic of the rowdy frontier period of Lampasas. Touting itself as the "Saratoga of the South," Lampasas had shed its violent past and courted tourists. The Gulf, Colorado, and Santa Fe Railroad had reached Lampasas in 1882, and the luxurious, 200-room Park Hotel was opened in 1883. A mule-drawn streetcar brought vacationers from the depot to the imposing Victorian hostelry adjacent to the curative waters on the southern edge of town. Another hotel was built, along with a fine opera house and new commercial structures. Pink Higgins—Indian fighter, feudist, mankiller—was the most intimidating reminder of the wild old days, and Lampasas of the 1890s regarded him more with disapproval than nostalgia. The trial for cattle theft was held in district court in Lampasas in November 1891, and the jury delivered a guilty verdict. Pink was sentenced to two years in the state penitentiary.[14]

Opened in 1849, the penitentiary at Huntsville became overcrowded during the crackdown on outlawry in the 1870s by Texas Rangers and local officers. To handle the overflow, a larger facility was constructed at Rusk in East Texas. The main building of the Rusk Penitentiary was a massive cellblock designed to hold 1,056 inmates. Pink's conviction and sentence was upheld on January 16, 1892, and his confinement dated from that point. He was jailed for a few weeks in Lampasas, then delivered to Rusk, arriving on February 17. Pink was measured at 6'1½" and 163 pounds, which indicates that imprisonment threw him off his feed. His health was judged "fair," and his education was evaluated as "limited." His habits were regarded as "intemperate," the only indication ever found by the author that Pink was much of a drinking man. It should be pointed out that an alternate definition of "intemperate" is "severe or violent," which may not have been intended by prison officials, but which is descriptive of Pink Higgins.[15]

Rusk inmates were clad in blue and white striped suits. They were marched to meals, work, and cells in lockstep, single-file with right hand on the shoulder of the man in front. Meals were eaten in silence. Strict discipline was maintained through solitary confinement, bread and water diets, or whippings with a three-foot leather strap.

Apparently Pink's incarceration brought his father and his sons, Cullen and Tom, to East Texas. Cullen attended Kilgore Business College, while Tom enrolled in Tyler Commercial College.[16] ("College" was a loose term among educational institutions of the 1890s.) Tyler was a little more than forty miles northwest of Rusk, and Kilgore was about the same distance to the northeast. John Higgins many have stayed in Tyler with his younger grandson. Both Tyler and Kilgore, of course, were within a short railroad visit of the Rusk Penitentiary.

Perhaps bolstered by the visits of family members, Pink

Rear view of the east wing of the cell block of the Rusk Penitentiary.
(Photo by Karon O'Neal)

proved to be an orderly prisoner. Confinement must have been an especially claustrophobic experience for a man who had ridden the open range all of his life. But he made no escape attempts, and he did nothing to draw punishment from prison officials. Because of crowded conditions, prisoners who behaved well often were paroled after serving half of their sentence. Pink's friends submitted petitions on his behalf to

The Rusk Penitentiary

Pink spent nearly two years during the early 1890s at the Rusk Penitentiary in East Texas. Authorized in 1875 by the Texas Legislature to relieve overcrowding at the Huntsville Penitentiary, construction began at Rusk two years later. Convicts provided part of the labor, and the new facility began to receive prisoners in January 1883.

The seven-acre compound was enclosed by a twenty-foot-tall brick wall. Three large structures inside were built of sandstone and brick: a three-story administration building; a domestic building which housed the kitchen, dining hall, hospital, library, and chapel; and a two-story cell house. With 528 double-bunked cells, the cell house could accommodate more prisoners than the facility at Huntsville. In 1888—two years preceding Huntsville—a power plant provided electric lighting at the Rusk Penitentiary.

Inmates were expected to offset a portion of their incarceration costs through productive labor. Outside the walls were manufacturing shops, iron foundries, a blast furnace, a sawmill, a brick kiln, and an ice factory. Convicts produced bricks, ice, iron products, wagons, mattresses, brooms, lumber, and paint. Inmates also worked at nearby prison farms, raising vegetables, fruits and livestock, and at timber camps, cutting trees for the sawmill.

The Rusk Penitentiary closed in 1917, soon reopening as the Rusk State Hospital for mental patients. The prison walls were razed, but the massive old cell house is still utilized.

Governor J. S. Hogg, but the state's top official was a former district attorney and deputy sheriff who once had been wounded while trying to make an arrest. Pink languished at Rusk until November 16, 1893, when he finally received a full commutation of his sentence—exactly two months before his scheduled release.

Back in Lampasas County, Pink realized that hard feelings over the Horrell-Higgins feud remained tangible, with no end in sight to bitterness. (As late as the 1940s, when C. L. "Doc" Sonnichsen came to Lampasas to investigate the feud, some descendants did not want to talk and a few parties muttered thinly veiled warnings.)[17] As early as the 1880s Higgins partisans began to leave this poisonous atmosphere.

After returning home, Pink resumed his activities as a stockraiser to feed his growing family. His daughter Rocky now was old enough to accompany him on pasture rounds and open gates. Pink's little boy, Roy, suffered epileptic seizures. Pink took him to Fort Worth for medical help, but following an extended period of treatment Roy died.

Cullen also was in Fort Worth during the 1890s. He had decided to became an attorney. The common procedure was to read law under the guidance of an attorney, who then would endorse his pupil, enabling him to buy a license to practice law. Cullen Higgins may have read law in the office of Lampasas attorney Roy Walker.[18] Cullen acquired his license and was admitted to the bar.

The new lawyer opened his practice in Fort Worth. By the late 1890s Fort Worth was a bustling city of 25,000, and Cullen soon decided to find a smaller town where there were fewer lawyers. In 1899, the twenty-four-year-old attorney moved to Snyder. The son of a pioneer, Cullen was confident that he could make a future for himself in the growing West Texas community.

Pink, who now felt out of place in tame and civilized Lampasas County, also was drawn to West Texas, where the values and attitudes of his youth were still esteemed. In 1899 Pink hired on as a stock detective with the vast Spur Ranch.

Bustling Fort Worth during the 1890s, where Pink took his ailing son, Roy, for treatment, and where Cullen Higgins briefly practiced law.
(Author's collection)

6

Range Rider
for the Spurs

*"So I dropped on my knee, trying to get a bead on him,
and when he slowed down I let him have it."*

Pink describing his fight with Billy Standifer

BY THE LATTER YEARS of the nineteenth century, Lampasas
had become too civilized for men who had known the freedom
and exhilaration of frontier life. Although now entering middle age, many of the most rugged individuals restlessly left the
"Saratoga of the South" for the relatively uninhabited spaces
of West Texas.

There was a minor exodus to the northwest. One of the
first to go was Jess Standard, who had trailed cattle with Pink
and ridden with him through the feud. Standard's wife had
died young, but he had remarried and moved his new family

72

to a small spread outside Tuscola, south of Abilene. Billy
Standifer, whose father owned a mercantile in Lampasas,
became a cowboy. Drifting west, in the 1880s he worked as a
roundup boss for cattle baron C. C. Slaughter, then entered
law enforcement and won election as sheriff of Crosby County
in 1889. He would be considered an effective lawman.
Members of the Rasberry and Higdon families also migrated
from Lampasas to the northwest.[1]

Bill Wren, Pink's staunch friend, served as sheriff of
Lampasas County from 1892 to 1896. But Wren could not
resist the lure of newer country, and after leaving office he
moved his family to Scurry County. Pink was in his late forties
and had a houseful of children from his second marriage, but
he, too, felt the pull to the west. In 1899 Pink, leaving his
family for the time being at Higgins Gap, journeyed to sparsely
settled Kent County to explore possibilities. Cullen also came
out, moving to Snyder from Fort Worth to continue his legal

Bill Wren fought in the Horrell-Higgins feud, later served as sheriff of
Lampasas County, then moved to West Texas. He is buried in the Snyder
Cemetery.   **(Photo by Berri Hodges)**

career. Cullen's sister, Malinda, had married W. L. Taylor, and they stayed in Rumley, while Cullen's brother, Tom, also elected to remain in Lampasas County. But four years later Pink's brother-in-law and sister, Tom and Malinda Jane Terry, left Lampasas County, settling with their eight children about four miles west of Roby.[2]

When Pink followed the impulse of his pioneer ancestors and migrated west, he therefore had other family members and friends in the vicinity. Also in the neighborhood were men from Lampasas County who were not family or friends, and it would prove easy for the Higgins clan to become the object of enmity in their new home. And neither Pink nor his relatives and friends would be any more inclined to back down from trouble in West Texas than they had been in Lampasas County.

Pink began to build up a little spread on Catfish Creek (now known as White River) in the northwestern corner of Kent County near the eastern line of Garza County. The landscape was sandy, brushy, and harsh, but Catfish Creek would provide water for livestock. The area had few settlers, and there were no nearby towns. Clairemont, the county seat, was well over twenty miles away by poor roads. The nearest railroad connections were almost ninety miles distant: the Fort Worth and Denver, to the north, and the Texas and Pacific, to the south. If Pink was looking for wide-open, isolated rangeland similar to the home of his youth, he had found it on Catfish Creek.

Pink's property was squeezed in between the vast East and West pastures of the Spur Ranch. Organized by wealthy British investors in 1885, the Espuela ("Spur" in Spanish) Land and Cattle Company eventually fenced in a total of 569,120 acres in Kent, Dickens, Garza, and Crosby counties. The Spurs, as the big ranch was called, was divided into the East Pasture and West Pasture, which were connected by a narrow neck of land in northwestern Kent County. Pink's new home would be located just above this connecting point.

In 1889 the London board of directors appointed

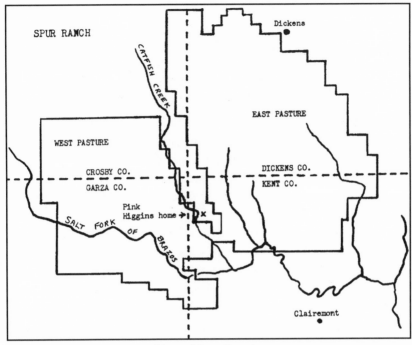

Map of Spur Ranch.

Scotsman Fred Horsbrugh as manager of their ranch, a position he would hold for fifteen years. Horsbrugh increased the
cattle herd to more than 54,000, and upgrading was begun by
purchasing 200 Hereford and Shorthorn bulls annually for six
years. By 1895 most Spur cattle had white faces. The horse
herd numbered about 800, with each cowboy assigned a
string of ten mounts. Numerous stock tanks were built, and
fifty-seven windmills eventually improved the Spur water sup-
ply. Often there were forty or more employees, who were
expected to work seven days a week, with three days at
Christmas the only holiday.[3]

Horsbrugh was popular and hard-working, but despite his
best efforts the Spur was consistently unprofitable. Range conditions often were poor because of frequent drought or prairie
fires. Cattle weakened by inadequate grazing died by the

thousands when winter blizzards struck. Hailstorms some-times dropped stones big enough to kill large numbers of calves, and calves also were the frequent prey of wolves.

In addition to regular losses from these causes, the Spurs—like large ranches throughout the West—was constantly raided by cattle thieves. Small operators felt that cutting out and branding a few strays would not cause a noticeable loss in a herd that numbered in the tens of thousands. Cowboys work-ing for a big spread often built up a little herd of their own by taking a few head from absentee owners. But small losses, when numerous enough and often enough, could cut deeply into the largest herd.

Spur rangeland was infiltrated by solitary riders who, if intercepted, claimed to be searching for a stray horse. A com-mon practice was to kill a mother cow in order to make off with an unbranded calf; the ranch lost not only a $10 calf, but also a $35 cow and the calves she would produce in future years. This cruel device was especially costly since rustlers usually picked out choice specimens.

Like other big spreads, the Spurs fenced in sections of state school land; if there were settlers on these small parcels,

Spur cowboys.

(Author's collection)

they usually sold out and departed when surrounded by a vast ranch property. But some bold operators took up school claims, thereby placing themselves in the midst of a great herd. If a rustler could secure and brand an average of a calf per week, his profits would be lucrative—and the losses to the ranch would be even greater. One man filed on school lands inside the West Pasture in the early 1890s. Settling inside Spur range with thirty-five head of cattle, this accomplished thief regularly

From Cow Servants to Cowlets

British stockholders and their wives often visited the Spurs. Cowboys tried to stay away from the well-dressed ladies and gentlemen, who persisted in calling them "cow servants."

The most frequent visitor was wealthy Scotsman John McNab, who disdained horseback in favor of touring the enormous ranch on foot. He set out on each expedition in proper London attire: business suit and cravat with starched collar and cuffs; stiff bowler hat; polished shoes; and an umbrella, which was not needed for rain protection but provided welcome shade from the withering Texas sun. Spur cowboys were asked by ranch manager Fred Horsbrugh not to shoot holes in McNab's umbrella or bowler.

Half-wild Spurs cattle became skittish at the unfamiliar sight of a pedestrian with an open umbrella, and when McNab was around the cowboys went on alert to head off stampedes. Since McNab usually got lost when he walked very far from headquarters, a cowboy always rode out of sight to "loose herd" him. When McNab became bewildered, the cowboy would appear as if by coincidence and offer to guide him.

Once Mrs. McNab and another stockholder's wife were observing a roundup at which bull calves were being branded, earmarked, and castrated.

"It is terrible to treat those little cowlets like that!" exclaimed one of the ladies.

"Ma'am, them's not cowlets," remarked a cowboy with a straight face. "Them's bullets."

sold about one hundred head annually. (After costing the Spurs an estimated $15,000 in stolen cattle, in 1901 the board of directors authorized Horsbrugh to buy him out.)

The Spurs joined the Northwest Texas Stock Raisers Association, formed for the purpose of protecting its membership from theft. The association assigned stock detectives to shipping points and to range duties, offered substantial rewards, and provided legal assistance. When rustlers were prosecuted, however, it often proved difficult to find twelve jurors who would convict a man of stealing from a vast, foreign-owned ranch. In 1890 a Spurs cowboy named Hosea gave chase to a horse thief who headed north, and Sheriff Billy Standifer helped apprehend the rustler. The Spurs board voted a $50 reward to Hosea, but Fred Horsbrugh also requested a reward for Sheriff Standifer. When Standifer's term expired, he was hired by several large ranches to work as a range detective.[4]

The Spurs was not one of the ranches which employed Standifer. Fred Horsbrugh continued to depend on the protection of the Northwest Texas Stock Raisers Association and the legal system. But beginning in 1896 cattle theft on the Spurs increased appreciably, and Horsbrugh began to consider employing range detectives on the Spurs. The most famous stock detective of the era was the notorious Tom Horn, who regularly rode the ranges of his Wyoming employers. Often Horn intimidated suspected rustlers into leaving the country. If intimidation failed to work, the thief frequently was gunned down. William Lewis, Fred Powell, Matt Rash, and Isom Dart were warned to leave the country, and when they did not they each were assassinated—by Horn, it was widely presumed. Horn's contemporaries understood his purpose: "He was given employment by some of the larger cattle outfits, to rid the country of rustlers and sheep men, to dispose of them in his own fashion; they called him a range rider."[5]

By 1898 Fred Horsbrugh decided that the Spurs needed its own range riders. He informed his board of directors that he was setting up a Protection Account, assuring them that "whatever I do spend in this direction will be small, I am sure, to the value that we have stolen from us every year now."[6] Horsbrugh contacted a Denver detective agency and arranged to have an operative sent to the Spurs. He would be paid $50 per month and mounted by the Spurs, and his identity would be known only to Horsbrugh and the agency in Denver.

In 1899 Horsbrugh had an opportunity to hire "the famous Standifer, who lately has been acquitted in the case in which he killed the worst thief we had down at Clairemont last year."[7] Working for ranches south of the Spurs, Standifer had pressured several suspected rustlers into leaving the country. By 1899 his success as a range rider had freed up some of his time, and he offered his services to the beleaguered Spurs. Horsbrugh agreed to pay him $40 per month from the Protection Account for part-time duties.

Horsbrugh also hired a man named Tynam as range rider. Tynam soon left the Spurs, however, and Horsbrugh replaced him with Pink Higgins. Pink had recently moved to Catfish Creek, he had worked with cattle all his life, and his reputation as a gunman certainly would intimidate any prudent rustler. Almost immediately "two families of well known thieves" departed for New Mexico, and by the end of the year Horsbrugh was so satisfied with the aggressive efforts of Higgins and Standifer that he released the undercover detective from Denver. By 1900 only two or three families of suspected rustlers still lived within the Spur fence, "and they are very careful of what they do." Horsbrugh happily reported that Standifer and Higgins "have already done us a great deal of good."[8]

A new type of "cattle leakage" began to occur when area settlers were offered $15 a head for yearlings, no questions asked, by cattle ranchers from another region. A number of suspects lived in dugouts in Pink's neighborhood, and he was instrumental in curtailing their activities and continuing the exodus toward New Mexico. In addition to a good wage, Pink—and Standifer—could draw supplies from the ranch store. The Spurs provided a little house for Pink, who moved his wife and children out in June 1900. Pink and Standifer more than earned their keep, as they continued to prove "very successful in putting down stealing," according to Horsbrugh.[9]

But there was trouble between the two range riders. Horsbrugh termed it "an old grievance." Clifford B. Jones, a later Spur manager, interviewed Pink and obtained details about the Standifer trouble: "Bad feeling had grown up between Higgins and Standifer and the latter's close friend, Bill McComas." Jones related that Standifer had come from the Lampasas area, and his sympathy with the Horrells laid the basis for his enmity with Higgins. Certainly a difference over the Horrell-Higgins feud would have provided abundant fuel for "an old grievance." A story was handed down that Pink once had pistol-whipped a friend of Standifer. W. J. Elliott, longtime employee of the Spurs, reminisced that Standifer had recently been divorced by his third wife, whose lawyer was young Cullen Higgins. Elliott speculated "that always after it was granted, Billy had a chip on his shoulder when Pink Higgins was near or his name mentioned." He added, "This might be only fancy on my part."[10]

Hard feelings grew when Pink began to suspect his fellow range detective of working for himself by "tying up a number of Spur calves found hobbled in the Spur West pasture." One of the houses on Pink's property was burned, and he suspected Standifer. Pink heard that Standifer, while drunk, "had said he would 'get him' the next time he saw him." When Pink did not respond to this second-hand challenge, apparently Standifer "got the mistaken notion that Higgins was afraid of him."[11]

Fred Horsbrugh determined to head off this escalating clash between two Spur employees who had been hired, in part, because of their reputations as dangerous gunmen. Horsbrugh confronted the problem directly, making it plain to his range riders that their jobs were on the line. "I made them both understand that they were no good to me if they were not friendly to each other, as their usefulness depended on their relations one to the other. They fully promised to make it all up and let bygones be bygones." Horsbrugh was satisfied that he had patched up the quarrel between his two capable range riders. "I thought I had the whole thing settled quietly," he stated.[12]

But the dispute flared again, in August 1902. Horsbrugh had no intention of allowing bad blood to boil over among Spur employees.

He fired Standifer first, then sought out Pink. By the time Horsbrugh confronted Pink, it was September and the fall term of school was about to start. With a house full of children, Pink asked permission to stay on until the end of September, so that he could arrange to move his family to a place where a school was available. (The previous year Pink had felt it necessary to take his two oldest daughters, Rocky and Ruby, to a Catholic school in Stanton, ninety miles to the southwest, for a term of schooling.) Horsbrugh was generous with an employee who had made a significant contribution to the ranch. "I told him a month did not matter."[13]

Before the end of the month, however, Standifer returned to the neighborhood, triggering Pink's keen survival instincts. Pink later told Charles Jones that one night he heard a coyote howl, but when his hounds did not give chase, he concluded that Standifer might be the "coyote," waiting outside for Higgins to appear in a doorway. Each morning Pink drove his saddle horses into the corral, and when he found horse tracks nearby he decided that Standifer or Bill McComas was spying on his habits, or setting up an ambush.

For two days Pink stayed inside the house. But Pink's nature would not allow him, as he told Charles Jones, to "live holed up like a rat any longer." Indeed, Horsbrugh understood that the shooting was "a premeditated (and mutually arranged for) duel."[14]

Early on Wednesday morning, October 1, 1902, Pink saddled Sandy, his favorite mount, and rammed his Winchester into the boot. A short distance from his house, Pink

Our Lady of Mercy Academy

When Pink moved his family from Lampasas County to the Spur Ranch, there were no nearby schools for his children to attend. Nearly one hundred miles to the southwest, however, West Texas boasted a quality educational institution in the little railroad town of Stanton.

One of the remaining structures of Our Lady of Mercy Academy in Stanton, where Pink enrolled two of his daughters.
(Courtesy Martin County Historical Society, Stanton)

German Catholic settlers founded Marienfeld ("Field of Mary") at a section station of the Texas and Pacific in 1881. Three years later Marienfeld became the seat of newly organized Martin County, and in 1890 the town's name was changed to Stanton in honor of Edwin M. Stanton, Abraham Lincoln's secretary of war. In 1883, atop a hill on the northern outskirts of town, a Carmelite monastery was opened, but the monks left four years later. Next the Sisters of Divine Providence established a parochial school at the monastery site, but this endeavor lasted only a year.

In 1894 the Catholic structures were reoccupied by Mother M. Berchman Kast, a few other nuns (the "Angels of Mercy") and sixteen students. Our Lady of Mercy Academy

(continued on next page)

(continued from previous page)

soon became known as a quality boarding school that would educate more than 2,000 students over the next four decades.

Pink Higgins, like many frontiersmen, viewed education as an essential tool for equipping his children to rise economically and socially. Probably in 1900, the first year his family spent in West Texas, Pink placed his two oldest girls, Rocky Rivers and Ruby Lake, in Our Lady of Mercy Academy.

It is likely that Pink brought his daughters

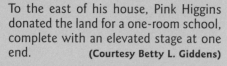

To the east of his house, Pink Higgins donated the land for a one-room school, complete with an elevated stage at one end. **(Courtesy Betty L. Giddens)**

by wagon to Colorado City, about fifty miles south of his home, then accompanied them another fifty miles westward on a Texas and Pacific train. There were five adobe and frame structures atop the old convent hill: a church, a classroom building, a boys' dormitory, a two-story girls' dorm, and a two-story residence (the original monastery building) for the Angels of Mercy.

Rocky and Ruby studied under the Angels of Mercy for a year. They did not return after summer vacation, as Pink sought closer educational opportunities that would not separate his family. Pink later donated a couple of acres of his own Kent County land for a rural school, and his children eventually picked up more schooling than he had. A tornado destroyed most of Our Lady of Mercy Academy in 1938, and the school closed after forty-four years of operation. The Angels of Mercy residence and ruins of the other buildings are still on the hill, and the two-story residence is being restored as of this writing (1998).

encountered Standifer. Both men were riding in the same general direction, with Standifer on Pink's right. Pink felt certain that Standifer would dismount to use his horse for cover, just as Pink intended to utilize Sandy.

"So I made up my mind to keep my eye on his left foot," related Pink, "and the minute that foot left the stirrup I would get off and go for my gun."[15]

Warily the two adversaries rode closer, until they were separated by a distance later measured at sixty-two paces. Suddenly, Standifer's left boot left the stirrup, and Pink instantly slipped out of the saddle, pulling at his Winchester as he stood behind Sandy. He had a hard time clearing his rifle from its scabbard, and as he finally cocked and leveled the weapon, Standifer fired a shot.

The bullet hit Sandy. The stricken animal slammed into Pink, then bolted. Pink's shot went wild as he was knocked off-balance. "I always hated to lose the first shot," lamented Pink to Charles Jones.

Standifer's horse also had run away because of the gunfire, leaving him with no protection. "Standifer was shooting, but he was jumping around like a Comanche and his shots were going wild. He was sideways to me, and so then I knew I had to shoot mighty accurate to hit him. I knew he couldn't do any good with his gun till he stopped jumping. So I dropped on my knee, trying to get a bead on him, and when he slowed down I let him have it. I knew I had got him when the dust flew out of his sleeve above the elbow and he started to buckle. He dropped his gun into the crook of his other arm and tried to trot off. I called to him, saying if he had had enough I wouldn't shoot again and would come to him, but he fell face forward, his feet flopped up, and he didn't speak."[16]

The bullet had ripped through Standifer's arm and ranged into his torso, inflicting a fatal wound. Pink had seen the bullet strike his arm, but he was afraid Standifer was playing possum. Pink caught up with Sandy, bleeding badly from a wound in the withers, and rode toward his home for an uninjured mount.

Back at the house, Lena Higgins sent one of her daughters, Bonnie Bay, up to the roof with a pair of field glasses. The sound of gunfire halted, and Bonnie Bay peered intently through the glasses. "I can't see anything but Daddy," she finally announced, "and he is coming this way in a lope."

Just before reaching the corral, Sandy dropped dead. Pink saddled another horse and set out toward Clairemont. When he reached a ranch house with a telephone, he called Sheriff N. N. Rodgers and said he thought he had killed Standifer. Higgins relished recounting the veteran sheriff's reply: "He said if I wasn't sure I had better go back and finish."[17]

Higgins rode into Clairemont and turned himself in to the sheriff. At the scene of the shooting it was apparent that the fight had been fair. Pink was gratified to receive telegrams and letters from friends in various locales, offering to go on his bond. But bail was not necessary. A grand jury convened and, acknowledging the time-honored Western tradition of self-defense, exonerated Pink of any crime.

Fred Horsbrugh was in Clairemont when the telephone call came about the fight. Five days later, he wrote an account to the London office: "I regret to report a killing that took place on our range a few days ago." Horsbrugh described the event and his efforts to avert trouble. He explained that Higgins would be able to claim self-defense. "But, of course, the return of Standifer could have only one meaning for a jury. They were both fearless, determined men, and each had similar trouble before; and they were really the means of scaring out some of the worst cow-thieves we had."[18]

Because Pink was such an effective range rider, and since Standifer no longer would cause conflict, Horsbrugh took the practical step of rehiring Higgins. Equally pragmatic was the replacement for N. N. Rodgers, Sheriff B. F. Roy, who placed Pink's gun on the side of the law by appointing him a deputy sheriff of Kent County.

The shooting site, located on the edge of Pink's land, became known as "Standifer's Thicket." Standifer was buried nearby. When Pink was asked if the grave was located where he fell, an unsympathetic Pink exclaimed, "Damn him, no! Do you think I'd let him stay on my place?"[19]

Billy Standifer's headstone proclaims that he was "KILLED BY PINK HIGGINS."
(Photo by Karon O'Neal)

7

Pink's
Final Years

*"He was a man true to his friends, true to his ideals,
and at all times a man among men."*

Pink Higgins obituary

AFTER KILLING BILLY STANDIFER, Pink enjoyed the most peaceful decade of his life. Perhaps he mellowed a bit, but it was just as likely that potential adversaries were not foolish enough to push him very far.

For a few years following the death of Standifer, Pink continued to thwart rustling on the Spurs range. Working with Jeff Harkey, an inspector for the Northwest Texas Cattle Raisers Association, Pink traced some stolen calves to a nester's school land claim inside the Kent County range of the Spurs. The suspected rustler was not at home, but his wife swore that the calves belonged to them. Pink and Harkey drove the calves to some nearby Spur cows. "Two of the calves sucked then and there," reported Horsbrugh. "Higgins says that he and his family can swear to several other calves being 'Spur' property." Two suspected thieves were indicted by a grand jury in Clairemont. No Kent County jury had ever convicted anyone of stealing from the foreign-owned Spurs. But Spurs lawyers succeeded in having the trial moved to Snyder in Scurry County, where a conviction was obtained. After thousands of Spur calves had been marked with other brands, a conviction finally had resulted. More convictions would follow, and the rustling decline engineered by Pink Higgins accelerated.[1]

Pink's employment as a range detective for the Spurs ended within a few years. The Board of the Espuela Land and Cattle Company, after more than two decades of unprofitable operations, commissioned Fred Horsbrugh to find a buyer. Horsbrugh interested the S. M. Swenson Company in the Spurs, and transactions were completed in 1907. The Swenson syndicate acquired title to 437,670 acres of land, along with 30,000 cattle and horses. The new owners laid out the townsite of Spur and other communities, promoted a railroad into Spur, and began selling parcels of land to farmers and small ranchers. A sizeable ranch was maintained in part of the old West Pasture, but the Swenson "SMS" brand was used on the cattle. Offices of the Swenson Land and Cattle Company were housed in a new building in Stamford.

No longer a range rider, Pink may have bought a parcel of the old Spurs to add to his property, now known as "Catfish Ranch." In 1907 Pink built a board-and-batten house on his place, hauling in lumber on his wagon. There also were corrals and outbuildings. Pink ran as many as one hundred head of cattle on Catfish Ranch, and he grew feed and peanuts. By the time of his death in 1913, Pink had accumulated "real and personal property of the probable value of Twenty Thousand Dollars." Part of this estimated $20,000 may have been a life insurance policy. Although Pink's oldest son was a lawyer,

Pink never wrote a will, and Cullen had to settle his affairs after his death on behalf of the widowed Lena Higgins. At the time of his death Pink and two other men were involved in a lawsuit against the Globe Fire Insurance Company.[2]

In 1912 Pink was sued by John Snowden over a 160-acre parcel of land. Snowden was the killer of Jeff Hardin, younger brother of gunfighter John Wesley Hardin and a dangerous character in his own right. Like Pink, Jeff Hardin rode

"Pink Higgins Will Bring His Own Goats"

Pink was hired by ranchers in the Pecos area, about two hundred miles southwest of his home. Plagued by rustlers, the ranchers hoped that Pink could provide a rapid solution. Soon Pink apprehended a rustler skinning a stolen cow, and he tied the green hide around the thief. For a day or so the stinking, bloody hide dried out and tightened around the miserable rustler. When Pink finally turned the thief over to the sheriff, the rustler gasped that he wished "he had killed me."

"Why didn't you?" asked the sheriff, as though the idea was a good one.

"He's a walking advertisement," said Pink, pointing out that word would quickly spread among the rustlers. Apparently it did, and Pink headed home with a fee in his pocket.

Pink's formidable reputation cost him another fee, according to Bob Terry. A rancher named Cox was losing goats to Mexicans who lived nearby. Cox sought out the goat rustlers and told them he intended to hire Pink Higgins to stop their thievery. They knew that Pink would do anything necessary to stop them. "Pink Higgins will bring his own goats," declared one thief, knowing that he would be lucky if Pink simply manufactured evidence instead of resorting to gunplay. With the threat of Pink Higgins hanging over them, the Mexicans promptly left the country.

Pink Higgins late in life, wearing lace-up boots on a snowy day in West Texas. It is believed that he is standing beside the board-and-batten house he built on his Catfish Ranch in 1907.

(Courtesy Betty L. Giddens)

as a stock detective for at least one of the big ranches in the region, and in 1901 he killed a cattle thief. Soon afterward Jeff and Snowden encountered each other in Clairemont at the livery stable of Benjamin Hardin, Jeff's first cousin and Snowden's father-in-law. Jeff and Snowden quarreled over the shooting, and Hardin supposedly threatened his cousin-in-law (there were no witnesses). Snowden shot Hardin to death, claimed self-defense, and did not stand trial.

When Snowden challenged Pink in court over a quarter-section of land, Pink's case was handled by his son, Cullen Higgins. Cullen successfully defended Pink's claim to the land, and Snowden wisely let the matter drop. John Snowden had proved that he could be a deadly gunman, but even at sixty-one, Pink Higgins was one of the most lethal shootists still alive in the West.[3]

By this time, however, Pink was regarded not only with respect, but with a certain amount of nostalgic affection. Known as a courageous old frontiersman, he enjoyed a wide network of friends, he was a strong family man, and "he was typical of real western manhood," enthused a reporter for *The Texas Spur*, the Spur newspaper. In Spur and elsewhere he was called "Uncle Pink."

Pink's home was thirteen miles southwest of Spur, and after the community was organized in 1909, it was the nearest town to the Higgins place. The family traded in Spur, regularly coming to town on Saturdays, like most other farmers and ranchers. Indeed, on the Saturday afternoon preceding his death, "he and his family were in Spur greeting their friends."[4]

Charles A. Jones was employed by the Swenson syndicate in 1907 to carry out their program of land promotion and sales. Jones was fascinated by the now-legendary Pink Higgins. Visiting with Pink as often as possible, Jones found him completely willing to talk about his various shooting scrapes, including the Standifer killing.

"With anyone who was interested, Higgins would discuss this shooting just as though it had been a wolf hunt, and with no more feeling, which is understandable enough when one considers that a human wolf was the victim."[5]

Conversations with other men who had been forced to kill had convinced Jones that they were usually plagued with remorse. "There was nothing of this about Pink Higgins," stated Jones. "He had it to do, and he did it, and that was all there was to it—no regrets, no cause for any."

Wanting his wife "to meet Pink and his fine family," Jones took her along on one of his visits to the Higgins home. Jones asked Pink to discuss the Standifer troubles, as well as the feud in Lampasas County. As Pink matter-of-factly described his lethal adventures, his handicapped daughter came over, and he pulled her into his lap and gently stroked her hair.

Mrs. Jones was taken aback by Pink's list of shootings, but he won her over with his obvious devotion to his family. Mentioning to Mrs. Jones that he had been indicted in Lampasas for killing fourteen men, he said "that it got so down there that if any man was found shot to death or had disappeared everybody said, 'Pink Higgins did it.'"

"Now, Mrs. Jones," added Pink reassuringly, "I didn't kill all them men—but then again I got some that wasn't on the bill, so I guess it just about evens up."

Asked to manage another Swenson property in 1913, Charles Jones' replacement was his son, Dr. Clifford B. Jones, who worked as manager of the SMS until 1938, when he was elected president of Texas Technological College in Lubbock. Along with his father, Clifford had been captivated by Pink, and accumulated extensive notes on Higgins. Clifford calculated

Snakebit!

Texas cattle ranges were infested with rattlesnakes, but with medical care largely unavailable on the frontier, cowboys had to resort to folk cures. In Lampasas County, Pink once was bitten through his boot top by a rattler with seventeen buttons. He kicked the snake off his boot, then tied a cord just below his knee. Pink took a knife and split three chickens down the back. When the chickens were applied to the wound, they turned green as the venom was pulled from Pink's leg. Like most Texas cattlemen, Pink was more afraid of skunks ("hydrophobia cats") than of rattlesnakes.

As the years passed, Pink picked up other snakebite remedies. He used one in November 1913, when his hired hand on the Catfish Ranch, a man named Bond, was bitten by a rattler with eleven buttons. When Pink soon afterward came into Spur to renew his newspaper subscription, *The Texas Spur* reported the incident.

"Uncle Pink immediately secured two shotgun shells from which he extracted the powder, which was bound to the wound after it had been properly bruised. On this he then poured coal oil and after an hour or two Mr. Bond was feeling as well as usual and returned to work."

No chickens had to be sacrificed, and *The Texas Spur* was impressed with the results: "This is a simple remedy for snakebites and our many readers should remember this in such emergency cases."

that Pink had "removed in personal encounter an even dozen human beings from this world and that a clear conscience makes him entirely willing to tell you, in that modest way of his, of these several killings."

Pink's attitude was the same as that of the Prince of the Pistoleers, Wild Bill Hickok: "As to killing, I never think much about it. I don't believe in ghosts, and I don't keep the lights burning all night to keep them away. That's because I'm not a murderer. It is the other man or me in a fight, and I don't stop to think—is it a sin to do this thing? And after it is over, what's the use of disturbing the mind?"[6] Pink's mind remained serenely undisturbed.

Rachel Ellis, daughter of a Spur Ranch employee, later told Elmer Kelton that Pink "freely admitted a number of killings and said that they were all justified." She emphasized that Pink "was a kind and thoughtful neighbor, whatever his past." Pink endeared himself to Rachel when he encountered her on the road with her father. She was riding a mule sidesaddle, and Pink told her father that he should be proud, because none of the Higgins daughters could ride a mule.[7]

Pink lost his parents during his fifties. His father, John Holcomb Higgins, died on December 30, 1903, less than three weeks before his eighty-first

Malinda Higgins Terry, sister of Pink Higgins.
(Courtesy Bob Terry)

The parents of Pink Higgins, John and Hester, lived into their eighties and were buried side by side at Rock Church Cemetery east of Lampasas.

(Photo by Karon O'Neal)

At the base of John Higgins' grave a stone was placed commemorating his service in the Confederate Army.

(Photo by Karon O'Neal)

birthday. John passed away in Austin, perhaps seeking medical care there, but he was brought back to Lampasas County and buried at Rock Church Cemetery, near the home of his daughter, with whom his wife lived.

When Pink returned to Lampasas to settle the estate of his father in January 1904, he was greeted with the respect accorded a noted pioneer. On Tuesday, January 11, just before boarding a train for Dallas and points west, Pink, accompanied by his son, Tom, visited the office of the *Lampasas Leader*. Pleased at the visit, the *Leader* editor reminded readers that Pink "was once one of the best known men in this section," and that he "has many friends in this section." (He probably had a few enemies, too.) Waxing nostalgic over the county's frontier period, the editor added: "He is one of the typical frontiersmen, and looks today as if he would enjoy a bout with Indians."[8]

Hester Higgins survived her husband by more than five years, dying at the age of eighty-two in Lampasas County on February 22, 1909. She was laid to rest beside John at Rock Church Cemetery.[9] Pink's mother was a devout Baptist who had insisted that her children read the Bible. Pink was said to have read the Bible cover to cover three times, but he never joined a church. A year or so after his mother died, however, Pink attended a service conducted in Spur's Methodist tabernacle—a roofed meeting-place with benches but no walls—by a Baptist minister, Reverend Fern Self. Pink announced his conversion and was baptized. When he encountered a circuit preacher in Clairemont, he asked the parson to stay in town until he could make a round trip to Catfish Creek. As rapidly as possible, Pink returned to Clairemont with four children as candidates for baptism. Although Lena was a Methodist, she had to be pleased that her gunfighting husband had made a religious committment.[10]

In her late teens, Rocky Higgins went to work for Cullen in his law office. Bright and capable, she traveled with Cullen to various courthouses for days at a time, and she also worked as a court clerk. When Pink and Lena were gone somewhere, Rocky was proud to be "head boss" over her sisters at home. Rocky fell in love with Emmett Johnson, son of Scurry County cattle baron Billy Johnson, and they married in 1907. For a time Ruby was courted by Emmett's younger brother, Sidney Johnson. But Sidney was not as likeable as the affable Emmett, and Pink opposed the match. Ruby and Sidney later found other spouses, but Ruby always would hold a soft spot for her first sweetheart.

Pink's daughters sometimes left their isolated home to visit friends for a day or two; Rocky hunted rabbits on one such trip, while Bonnie once had to help her hosts fight a prairie fire with quilts, suffering a blistered face and shredded clothing. Tom Higgins enjoyed this lively bunch, periodically traveling from Lampasas to visit Cullen and Pink and his half-sisters. (Tom became so fond of Lena that he made the journey to her bedside when she lay dying in 1937.)

Pink would not enjoy the lengthy lifespan of his parents. He had good genes, but he had gained weight, and he had led a hard life. On a cold Thursday morning, December 18, 1913, Pink arose to start a fire in the fireplace of his little house on Catfish Creek. Suddenly, he was wracked by a massive heart attack, and he dropped dead on his hearth. It was a curiously peaceful demise for a veteran of so many violent encounters. Despite warriors, rustlers, personal enemies, a bloody range war, and the dangers and hardships of frontier life, Pink Higgins had survived for sixty-two years in a dangerous land.

Al Bingham, a cowboy for the Spurs, rode to Pink's house to help prepare him for burial. Bingham had heard that Pink was scarred from head to toe from a lifetime of fighting, but he could find only a small scar above one wrist.[11]

Pink's funeral was not held until Sunday, December 21, perhaps to give his large family time to assemble. Services and burial took place in Spur. The final date carved on his gravestone was December 21, 1913, which was the day of his burial, not his death.

"We knew Uncle Pink personally and intimately, loved and appreciated him as a real man," lamented the editor of *The Texas Spur*. "He was a man true to his friends, true to his

No Greater Love

Throughout their courtship, Rocky Higgins tried to persuade Emmett Johnson to stop smoking cigarettes. In 1906 they became engaged, by correspondence (he was working on his father's ranch property twenty-five miles from Snyder, while she was at home on Catfish Creek or working in court at Clairemont or elsewhere). Rocky was elated in November 1906 when a letter from Emmett arrived with a packet of Wheat Straw cigarette papers stuffed inside the envelope. He wrote on the first paper, "Deserted for the love of you."

Emmett Johnson promised his fiancee, Rocky Higgins, that he would stop smoking, and as proof he mailed her his Wheat Straw cigarette papers, which she kept all of her life. **(Courtesy Betty L. Giddens)**

Rocky wrote back that she "shed tears of joy" over the gesture, while urging him to "keep his resolution to never smoke again." In her next letter she reported that her sister, Ruby, and Emmett's sister and brother-in-law, Gladys and Ed Sims, had presented her with a sack of "tobacco to smoke with my papers." Rocky teasingly announced her intention "to make them eat that tobacco next time I see them."

She closed a subsequent letter with a promise: "If you haven't smoked yet I owe you 50 kisses." Emmett, having licked his habit, felt free to answer: "P. S. I haven't smoked yet. Send me those kisses."

Wedding photo of Emmett Johnson and pretty Rocky Higgins.
(Courtesy Betty L. Giddens)

Mr. and Mrs. Pink Higgins,

request your presence at the marriage of their

daughter,

Rockie Rivers,

to

Mr. William Emmett Johnson,

at the home of Judge Cullen C. Higgins,

Snyder, Texas,

Sunday evening, May fifth, One Thousand

Nine Hundred and Seven,

at five o'clock.

Wedding invitation for Rockie Rivers Higgins (at different times she also spelled her name "Rocky" and "Rockye") and Emmett Johnson.

(Courtesy Betty L. Giddens)

ideals, and at all times he was a man among men." The fact that he "promoted justice and the effectual service rendered to the country and to civilization by Uncle Pink Higgins will be long remembered and his name honored by Texas citizenship."[12]

During the final years of his life there was a great deal that Pink Higgins could have regarded with satisfaction. Even though he had acquired little education or polish, even though he never held a position of prominence or influence, even though he never accumulated wealth, Pink Higgins command-ed widespread respect. He had spent his life among people who valued physical strength, skill with weapons, and sheer courage. Pink was a big man, strong and impressive in appear-ance. He was an expert with firearms, as he proved repeated-ly throughout his lifetime. He feared no man, and even after reaching middle age he accepted another life-and-death chal-lenge, then added to his intimidating list of victims. Widely known as a dangerous man if aroused, Pink was treated with deference and respect. He had led an existence that later gen-erations would regard as romantic: frontiersman, cowboy, trail driver, Indian fighter, range detective, shootist.

Pink was the devoted father of nine children, and by the time of his death he could take pride in his offspring. His old-est son, Cullen, had become a respected district attorney and district judge, and was building a successful and prosperous legal practice. As a parent Pink had stressed the need for edu-cation, and he had donated land for a rural school. Surely he was gratified when his second oldest son, Tom, taught for sev-eral years in Lampasas County. Tom also worked as a survey-or for a decade for the U. S. Reclamation Service, and not long before Pink's death, Tom was admitted to the bar. Rocky Rivers Higgins married Emmett Johnson, son of the Snyder area's most prominent cattleman. Other daughters married well, and before he died Pink was able to enjoy several grand-children.

The frontier had ended and Pink's children had become solid citizens of the twentieth century. Pink had not killed a

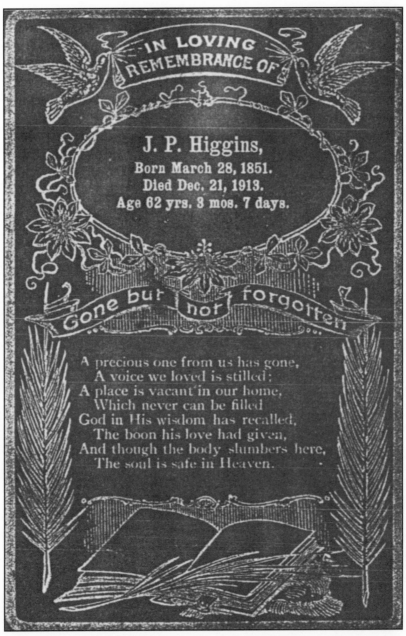

Funeral card distributed at Pink's funeral ("December 21" is the date of the funeral; he died three days earlier). These cards were printed on thick cardboard. The lettering was gold on a black background. (The author has an identical card—only the name and dates are different—from the funeral of his great-grandfather, who died in 1912.)   **(Courtesy Betty L. Giddens)**

man since 1902, and by the time of his own death in 1913, he undoubtedly expected that his offspring would be able to avoid the violence that had marked his life. But frontier attitudes still prevailed among many West Texans, and even before Pink died, a series of events began which would result in tragic bloodshed for the Higgins family.

Pink was buried in the cemetery at Spur. Curiously, the date of his burial (December 21) was placed on his stone, rather than the date of his death (December 18).   **(Photo by Karon O'Neal)**

8

A New Round of Violence Begins

*"I am counted a pretty good shot
with a Winchester, a crack shot."*

Will Luman testimony about killing Joshua Bostick

THREE YEARS BEFORE THE DEATH of Pink Higgins, a cattle theft charge set in motion events that triggered bitter resentment and a series of killings among men who were every bit as dangerous as the Lampasas County feudists of the 1870s. Pink, always a magnet for lethal range troubles, died before events began to explode, but his oldest son, a pillar of the West Texas legal system, would become perilously involved.

In April 1910 Si Bostick was tried for cattle theft at the red sandstone courthouse in Clairemont, seat of Kent County. Bostick was the oldest son of Joshua F. Bostick, a tough cattleman who brought his family from Oklahoma to West Texas when Si was a boy. At the age of fifteen, while he was left in charge of younger siblings at the family home near Post, Si took a saddle horse and ran off to New Mexico. Even after he married and began a family, Si continued to flirt with trouble. When he moved his wife and children to Oklahoma, for example, Si soon had reason to flee for Texas, hiding for a time in the attic of his younger brother, Amos.[1]

When charged with stealing cattle in 1910, the testimony of friends such as Will Luman resulted in acquittal, even though Si Bostick may have been guilty. Four years later, another cattle theft case, involving Will Luman and Joshua Bostick, among others, resulted in the conviction of a man who probably was innocent.

On Sunday, January 11, 1914, a black cow was found shot and butchered on O Bar O range in southern Kent County. Jim and Tom Latham, who lived near the 100,000-acre ranch, discovered the carcass in a mesquite thicket while hunting stray cattle. (Many people would come to believe that the Latham brothers killed the cow and made off with the meat, then shifted the blame elsewhere.) On Monday the Lathams rode into Clairemont and told veteran Sheriff Ivy McCombs and Dock Howell, range boss of the O Bar O. The butchered animal was "a big black motley-faced cow," so notorious for her wildness that her horns had been broken off so that she would not hook the horses of the cowboys trying to herd her.[2]

The next day, Tuesday, Sheriff McCombs and Dock Howell rode to investigate the carcass, guided by the Lathams. Sid Johnson, who ran a nearby spread and who was a Kent County constable, came along, and so did Joshua F. Bostick, who now operated a spread at the Riverdale community in southern Kent County, and who also functioned as a deputy constable. At the site of the cow killing, Sheriff McCombs located horse and boot tracks. He pulled out his pocket knife, picked up a stick, and notched measurements of the tracks into the stick. Armed with this rather inexact evidence, Sheriff

McCombs and his posse followed the trail a few miles, toward the farm of Lee Rasberry at Cox Hollow.

Only a few days earlier, Rasberry had moved his family onto a small rented farm about ten or eleven miles south of Clairemont. The family had been living nearby in a tent while Rasberry worked for the O Bar O, but shortly after Christmas Lee loaded his wife and two children into his mule-drawn wagon for a visit to her family in Post. It was a two-day wagon ride to the west; her father, J. W. Luman, lived in Post, and her brother, Will Luman, lived a couple of miles outside town. The

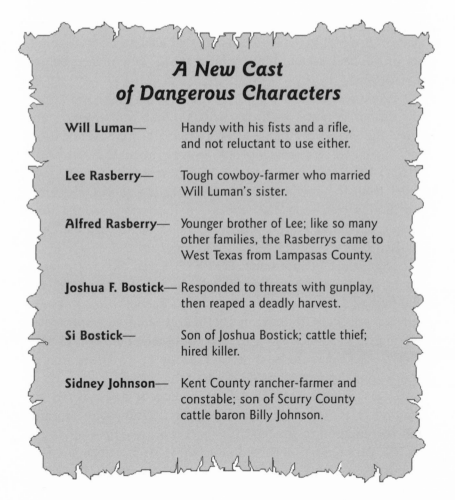

A New Cast of Dangerous Characters

Will Luman— Handy with his fists and a rifle, and not reluctant to use either.

Lee Rasberry— Tough cowboy-farmer who married Will Luman's sister.

Alfred Rasberry— Younger brother of Lee; like so many other families, the Rasberrys came to West Texas from Lampasas County.

Joshua F. Bostick— Responded to threats with gunplay, then reaped a deadly harvest.

Si Bostick— Son of Joshua Bostick; cattle thief; hired killer.

Sidney Johnson— Kent County rancher-farmer and constable; son of Scurry County cattle baron Billy Johnson.

Lumans presented gifts to their visitors on New Year's Day, 1914, and on Tuesday morning, January 6, when the Rasberrys were about to leave, Will Luman gave them the hindquarters of a freshly slaughtered beef. Will asked Lee to haul the forequarters into town to his father's house.

When the Rasberrys left Post, their wagon was loaded with a few live hogs as well as the beef hindquarters. Alfred, Lee's brother, came along to help with the farm.

After the two-day trek, the family moved into their new home on Thursday, January 8, and the next day Lee cut up the meat. Lee and his wife salted the beef, then packed it into two boxes. There were only two rooms in the little frame house; a makeshift closet was created by rigging a curtain across a corner of the back room, and the meat boxes were placed behind the curtain.

Five days later Sheriff McCombs and his posse rode up to the Rasberry farm. Rasberry shook hands all around, and when the sheriff announced the purpose of his investigation, Lee consented to a search of the house. The meat boxes and a .30-30 Winchester were found (Sid Johnson had dug a rifle bullet from the cow's carcass). Outside, the sheriff measured the shod hooves—not the tracks—of Rasberry's saddle horse against his marked stick, which he then checked against Lee's uplifted boot.

"She don't fit, does she, Ivy?"[3] observed one posse member of the hoof measurement. But Sheriff McCombs decided that he had sufficient evidence to bring Rasberry into custody. Lee did not want to leave his wife and children unprotected overnight, and since none of the posse members would stay, Sheriff McCombs agreeably told Rasberry to meet him in Clairemont the next day. With admirable integrity for a cattle thief—or perhaps because he was innocent and trusted the legal system—Lee rode into Clairemont Wednesday morning and surrendered to the sheriff.

A grand jury indicted Rasberry. His attorney, C. P. Woodruff, a highly regarded former district judge, succeeded in moving the trial to Anson, seat of Jones County. The trial was held in July 1914, and 130 pages of testimony provided only circumstantial evidence. No one disputed that the Rasberrys had brought meat from Post, although Joshua Bostick insisted that there was more meat than the couple had brought back from the Lumans. Judge Woodruff introduced testimony that freshly butchered meat had been seen at the Ratliff place, only a mile or so from the Rasberry farm. Nevertheless, the jury handed down a guilty verdict, and Rasberry was sentenced to two years in the penitentiary,

Judge Woodruff filed an appeal. In November the appeals court upheld the verdict, although one judge dissented, insisting that the evidence was "too inconclusive and uncertain." Rasberry, whose father-in-law had gone on his bond, finally went to prison, but within a few months he was pardoned by Governor James A. Ferguson.[4]

Lee Rasberry returned to his family filled with bitterness over his wrongful conviction. Reportedly he wrote Joshua Bostick and Sid Johnson, demanding that each man pay him $250 because of their role in sending him to prison. When the money was not forthcoming, Rasberry found Johnson in the Riverdale community, administered a beating, then collected $250.[5]

Joshua Bostick had no intention of surrendering $250 or taking a beating. Receiving threats from Rasberry, Bostick determined to take the initiative. On Wednesday, October 27, 1915, Bostick learned that Lee Rasberry was buying feed in Rotan, about ten miles southeast of Bostick's home. Bostick armed himself, saddled his horse, and headed for town with deadly intentions.

Bostick rode into Rotan from the north. Near the town's main intersection, where the north-south thoroughfare crossed the main east-west street, Bostick encountered Lee Rasberry and shot him. As Rasberry rolled over from the first bullet, Bostick shot him again, in the back, then snarled, "Now, damn you, tend to me."[6]

HIGGINS COUNTRY, 1899–1918

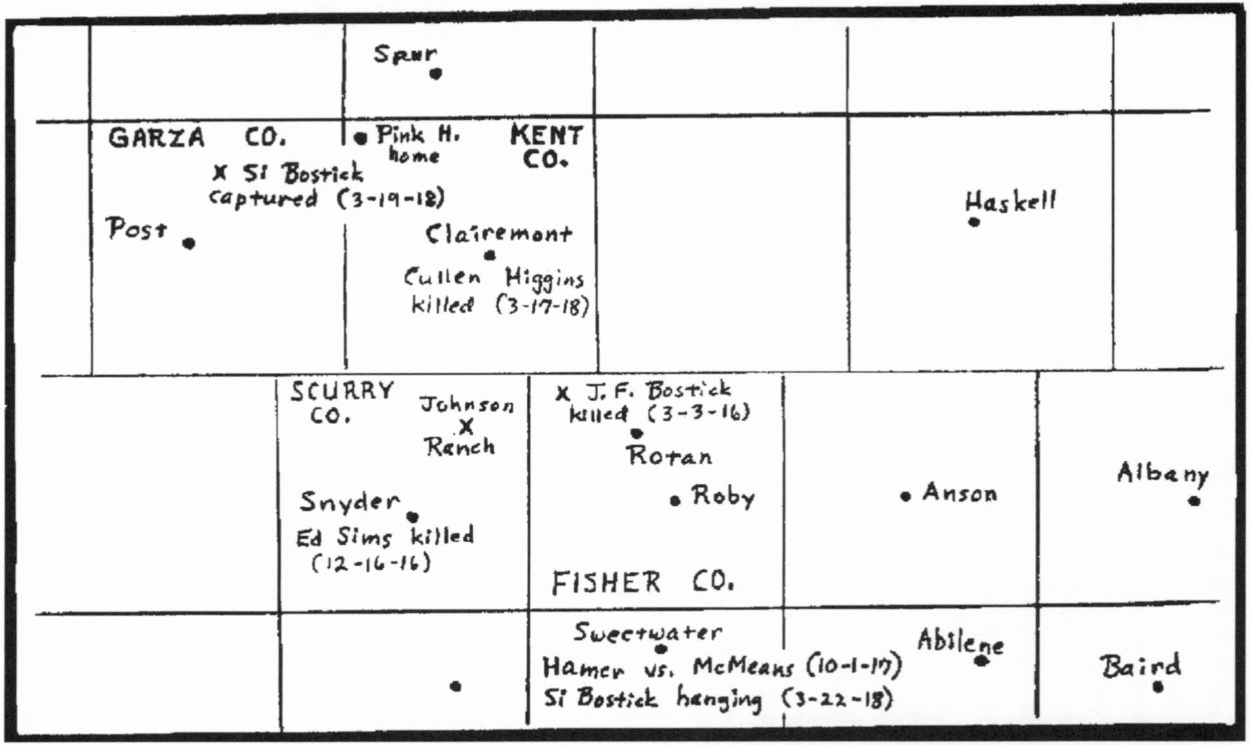

Spur •

GARZA CO.   KENT CO.

Pink H. home •

X Si Bostick captured (3-14-18)

Post •

Clairemont •

Cullen Higgins killed (3-17-18)

Haskell •

SCURRY CO.   Johnson X Ranch

Snyder •

Ed Sims killed (12-16-16)

X J. F. Bostick killed (3-3-16)

Rotan •

Roby •

Anson •

Albany •

FISHER CO.

Sweetwater •

Hamer vs. McMeans (10-1-17)

Si Bostick hanging (3-22-18)

Abilene •

Baird •

One version of the fatal shooting was that Rasberry was in a cafe when he heard that Bostick was riding into town. Rasberry came outside, pulling a pistol when he spotted Bostick. But Bostick fired first, fatally wounding Rasberry, who only managed one wild shot before collapsing. Rasberry's stray bullet apparently hit the big watch mounted atop the nearby watch shop of William Jasper Hull; years later, when the big watch was being moved for transfer to Corpus Christi, a bullet hole was found.

Another version held that Rasberry was armed with nothing more than a pocket knife. He was sitting in front of the feed store, whittling on a stick, when Bostick rode up and shot him in cold blood. But there are those who insist that Rasberry was found unarmed because his friends took his gun from his body so that Bostick would be charged with murder.

If someone hid Rasberry's pistol so that Bostick would be indicted for murder, the subterfuge was partially successful. A grand jury handed down an indictment for manslaughter, and the trial date was set for Monday, March 6, 1916. Trial testimony would have provided details of the fight, but the trial of Joshua Bostick was never held. Three days before his trial was scheduled to begin, Bostick was hunted down and killed by Lee Rasberry's brother and brother-in-law.

Alfred Rasberry understandably would want vengeance from the man who had shot his brother, and Will Luman had received numerous second- and third-hand threats from Bostick. Luman later would testify that he was told that Bostick "said I was a cow thief and my wife was a whore." In Post, where he lived, Luman was told by Ed Sims and Gee McMeans that Scurry County cattle baron Billy Johnson had heard (a third-hand threat!) that Bostick had been hired to kill him.[7]

Bostick supposedly was employed to kill Luman by Nick Bilby, half-owner of the O Bar O. It was understandable why Bilby might hire someone to deal with Luman. A couple of years earlier, while Lee Rasberry was being charged with the theft of the black O Bar O cow, Bilby was in the courthouse at Clairemont. The ranch owner grumbled "that the way he done fellows like Lee Rasberry wasn't to go to court with them, but was to put a rope around their neck and hang them to a cottonwood limb." Luman heard the remark about his brother-in-law and charged Bilby. With Alfred Rasberry looking on, Luman and Bilby "fought all over the room." A deputy sheriff finally broke up the courthouse brawl, hustling Luman and Rasberry outside, while the battered Bilby was carried to his hotel room.[8]

Will Luman was no stranger to trouble. At a country dance with his wife, Luman dodged a punch from a young man who called him an SOB, then dropped his adversary with one blow. There were other fistfights before he married. When tensions were high over the conviction of Lee Rasberry, Luman and Alfred Rasberry rode onto O Bar O range searching for a two-year-old horse. Suddenly, O Bar O range boss Dock Howell emerged from a draw. Howell pulled a revolver, but Luman instantly slid out of the saddle and, using his mount as a shield, leveled his Winchester.

"My God, think of my wife and babies," implored Howell, scrambling off his horse.[9]

There was an exchange of reassurances, and the danger passed. Then Alfred Rasberry suddenly rode over and wanted to whip Howell, shouting that "they swore a pack of lies on Lee and sent him to the pen." Although Luman persuaded his companion to leave Howell alone, Will was about to begin proving himself one of the most dangerous of men in a land of dangerous men.

Will Luman was born in Young County in 1888, the only boy among eight children. "I was just a little chunky, cotton-headed, heavy-set kid," he explained, "and my daddy always called me Dutch."[10] Later the family moved to Kent County, where J. W. Luman raised horses and mules and a few head of cattle. As a teenager, Dutch cowboyed for the big ranches in the area. He married a rancher's daughter named Faye

Edwards, fathered two children, and began his own little spread north of Post. His father moved into Post and opened a meat market, while one of his sisters married Lee Rasberry. When his sister's husband was sent to prison on an unjust charge of cattle theft, Luman took the injustice personally. Born and raised among the last generation of frontiersmen in West Texas, Luman was tough and unafraid of violence. Among his virtues was a devotion to family that was common to rural societies. He took Lee Rasberry's unfair conviction as a reflection on the entire family, and when Lee was killed by Joshua Bostick, Will's sister was left a widow with two children. For Will Luman, blood called to blood.

Luman tried to help his widowed sister and children. She married again, to a man named Boss Edwards, but Will continued to look after the livestock of his dead brother-in-law, and he sold some cattle for his sister. Late in February 1916, more than a week before Joshua Bostick was scheduled to stand trial for killing Lee Rasberry, Will left his home near Post to deliver the sale money to his sister and to hunt livestock. Alfred Rasberry, who had been staying with Will and with J. W. Luman, rode along to help, bringing a pump-action shotgun.

For a week Will Luman and Alfred Rasberry rode the countryside, rounding up horses and cattle that belonged to one or another of them, and staying with various relatives and friends. Some parties, however, suspected that the two riders were searching for Joshua Bostick, who wisely stayed at home.

It was general knowledge that Bostick had to appear in court at Roby on Monday morning. Instead of predictably leaving home for the twenty-mile trip to Roby on Sunday, Bostick decided to slip into Rotan on Friday morning, March 3, then proceed on to Roby, ten miles to the south. Although the best route was only about ten miles from his home into Rotan, Bostick took the precaution of using a roundabout trail. Apparently as a further precaution, he took his fifteen-year-old daughter, Lizzie, perhaps thinking—incorrectly—that he would not be killed in her presence. They traveled in a two-horse hack, and Bostick carried a rifle.

At about nine o'clock in the morning, the Bosticks encountered Will Luman and Alfred Rasberry. Joshua descended from his vehicle with his rifle.

"Look out, Will," shouted Rasberry.[11]

Luman later testified that Bostick got off one shot. Luman pulled his Winchester and slipped off the left side of his horse, but the frightened animal bolted, throwing his rider. Luman scrambled up, working his rifle. He drilled Bostick five times. Under oath Luman later would admit, "I am counted a pretty good shot with a Winchester, a crack shot."[12]

Riddled with five bullets, Bostick died on the spot. Fearing for her life, Lizzie Bostick picked up her father's rifle and threatened to shoot Luman and Rasberry if they approached her. (She later admitted that she did not know how to fire the gun.) Luman and Rasberry rode away without harming Lizzie: the killing seemed premeditated, but if they had murdered Bostick in cold blood, as they were accused, why did they not also murder the only eyewitness? Perhaps Bostick did try to fight back, and Luman and Rasberry felt that they could successfully plead self-defense.

When they rode off, Lizzie placed her father's hat over his face to keep off the sun. She pulled his watch and other valuables from his pockets. After half an hour, with no passersby on the lonely trail, Lizzie drove off to find help. About two miles from the killing site, the girl found a house, and a telephone call was placed to the Fisher County sheriff's office in Roby.[13]

A large posse searched for the killers Friday afternoon and Saturday. The trail of Luman and Rasberry led westward but disappeared after five miles, and telephone lines had been cut. Officials and citizens of Fisher and Kent counties posted a reward of $650, and Governor Ferguson added another $200 from the state. The officers knew the identity of the suspects and soon located and arrested Rasberry. Luman stopped by his home late Saturday night, then fled into New Mexico, traveling as far south as northern Mexico before reaching Arizona.

On March 8, 1916, Luman (*in absentia*) and Rasberry were indicted for murder. Rasberry was tried, convicted, and sentenced to twenty-five years in prison. His lawyers appealed the verdict, and the court of appeals eventually reversed the decision, which led to a new trial, scheduled for September 1917. In the meantime, Will Luman periodically slipped back into Post to see his wife, children, and other family members. Finally, officers caught Luman at Post in May 1917, arresting him just in time to bring him to trial with Rasberry.[14]

Cullen Higgins was appointed special prosecuting attorney against Luman. Pink Higgins' oldest son, by now regarded as one of the region's ablest attorneys, often was utilized as a special prosecutor. In September 1917, Higgins, the district attorney, and the defense attorneys agreed upon a change of venue, from Fisher County to Haskell County. Luman was tried in December 1917, but the case resulted in a hung jury. Another trial was scheduled for May 13, 1918. While between trial appearances, Luman was free on bail.

With Will Luman on the loose, witnesses and prosecutors had cause to feel unsafe. Indeed, by May 13, 1918, the tension would end in a death that extended the Higgins legacy.

9

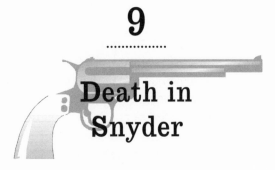

Death in
Snyder

*"You see what you have done.
I am unarmed."*

Ed Sims, after being shot

THE TOWN OF SNYDER was founded by Pete Snyder, a forty-two-year-old Union veteran of the Civil War who had prospected in Colorado and hauled freight in Kansas. By 1877 he was hauling buffalo hides from Texas hunters to Fort Worth, then returning to the plains with trade goods for the buffalo hunters. Pete Snyder established a crude trading post on the banks of Deep Creek, and in 1878 he brought lumber from Fort Worth to build a more substantial structure. A few hunters and settlers erected shelters near the trading post, and the rough little community was dubbed "Hide Town," "Robber's Roost," and "Snyder's Place." When Scurry County

114

was organized in 1884, "Snyder," located near the center of the new entity, was chosen as county seat. By the 1890s Snyder boasted two banks, two churches, two weekly newspapers, a cotton gin, and a growing population of more than six hundred.[1]

Cullen Higgins arrived in town in 1899 and began practicing law. Smart and industrious, Cullen prospered as an attorney and impressed almost everyone. "Now there was a great man," recalled Lena Hopson Powell, who had known Cullen during her girlhood, when he was a close friend of her father. "He was one of the handsomest men I have ever seen in my life. He looked a lot like [actor] Robert Young . . . , same sparkling brown eyes, same smile. And he had a million dollar personality."[2]

The popular Higgins became a community leader and a stalwart of Snyder's Methodist Church. "He was an open-minded Christian gentleman, a friend of every worthy interest, and was mindful at all times of the happiness and welfare of others," related the *Snyder Signal*. "He was a very busy lawyer, but always had time to render public service when needed."[3] He married Olive Smith, who was a few years older than Cullen, and they would have a son, Marshall, in 1910.

In 1902, at the age of twenty-six and after just three years in Snyder, Cullen won election as district attorney. After four years as district attorney, he was chosen as district judge. Only thirty years old in 1906, he was

Cullen C. Higgins, 1875-1918.
(Author's collection)

the youngest man ever to serve as district judge from Scurry County. (It was often told that the new judge decreed that anyone who wore spurs in his courtroom would be fined. The first to wear jingling spurs into the Higgins court was Pink, and the judge duly fined his father.) Judge Higgins distinguished himself as a jurist, but at the end of his four-year term he left the bench to return to private practice.[4]

For the rest of his life Higgins was respectfully called "Judge," and he practiced in all of the counties where he had served on the bench. Among his many clients was a prominent and powerful pioneer cattleman, W. A. "Billy" Johnson.

As a young trail driver, Billy Johnson brought a few cows and calves in 1878 to a section of state land about ten miles northeast of Snyder's Place. He found a spring on Ennis Creek and built a half dugout-half rock house, then began to put together a ranch that would eventually include forty-one deeded sections in Scurry and Kent counties. In 1884 he mar-

Pioneer cattle baron W. A. "Billy" Johnson, whose lawyer became Cullen Higgins and whose son married Rocky Higgins.

(Courtesy Betty L. Giddens)

Nanny Johnson, who married a pioneer rancher and became the mother of the affable Emmett, the short-lived Joe, and the volatile Sid and Gladys. **(Courtesy Betty L. Giddens)**

ried Nanny May Sims in Burnet County, and he added a room above the dugout. Their first son, Emmett, was born in 1885, and Joe followed two years later. After their third son, Sidney, was born in 1889, Billy built a two-story, L-shaped ranch house atop a rocky promontory with a splendid view. In 1891 a daughter, Gladys, was welcomed into the family. Billy taught all of his children, including Gladys, how to shoot, and the Johnson offspring embodied the courage and strong-mindedness of their pioneer parents. The Johnson children attended the Ennis Creek rural school, then went to Snyder High School.[5]

In 1902 fifteen-year-old Joe Johnson died of blood poisoning. His brother Emmett attended the New Mexico Military Institute in Roswell, entered ranching with his father, and in 1907 married Rocky Rivers Higgins, daughter of Pink and Lena. The couple had two children, and Emmett was a religious and kind-hearted man. Sidney also enrolled at the New Mexico Military Institute, then began ranching with his father. After courting Ruby Higgins for a time, Sidney married Ruth Smith, whose father was the first president of Snyder's First

Billy Johnson's ranch house north of Snyder in 1910. The family stands on the porch. From left: Gladys, Sid, Emmett, Joe, Billy and Nanny. Note the well in the yard. **(Courtesy Scurry County Museum, Snyder, Texas)**

National Bank, which Billy Johnson had helped found. Sidney and Ruth had a son, Weldon, but the couple later divorced.

While only fourteen, on August 31, 1905, Gladys married Ed Sims, a rancher from Garza County, just northwest of Scurry County. The young couple had two daughters, Helen, born in 1907, and Beverly, born in 1909,[6] but while Helen and Beverly Sims were still children the marriage became badly strained. By 1914 Gladys and the two girls had moved back to the Johnson Ranch, where Billy had erected a magnif-

The children of Billy and Nanny Johnson, ca. 1900. Seated, Emmett (born 1885). Standing, from left: Sidney (born 1889), Joe (born 1887, died in 1902 of blood poisoning), Gladys (born 1891).

(Courtesy Scurry County Museum, Snyder, Texas)

icent new home. Completed in 1910, the sixteen-room house boasted an intricate parquet floor in the parlor and oaken woodwork throughout the interior. Gladys and her daughters were welcomed back home, and when divorce proceedings commenced in 1916, Billy Johnson turned to Judge Cullen Higgins for legal counsel.

By this time Cullen's law office was in the second story of the First National Bank Building, where Billy Johnson had been president since 1907. On behalf of Gladys, Higgins filed for divorce at the Scurry County Courthouse, and he also filed an injunction against Ed Sims regarding the couple's property and custody of the children. "A good deal of excitement and bitter feeling was aroused on account of this injunction," reported a newspaper, and "various other mishaps and unpleasantness" ensued.[7]

Sims filed his own suit for divorce in Garza County, where the couple had lived on his ranch. The case was scheduled to be heard on Tuesday morning, July 25, 1916, while the District Court was in session at Post, the seat of Garza County. Cullen Higgins lined up ten to fifteen possible witnesses for Gladys. A similar number of witnesses was gathered for Ed Sims, and by Monday morning almost all parties had assembled in Post. Gladys and Ed bitterly expressed their hard feelings toward each other, and their friends joined in the seething hostilities.

Although it was a decade and a half into the twentieth century, these West Texans still bristled with the violent impulses of the frontiersmen who had settled the region only

The sixteen-room Johnson ranch house, built in 1910 of concrete blocks. Located twelve miles northeast of Snyder, this splendid house faces east.
(Photo by Berri Hodges)

a generation earlier. On the eve of their courtroom confrontation, Gladys and Ed came heeled, and so did their supporters. Little was done to conceal the dangerous fact "that each side was well armed, having pistols, Winchesters, and shotguns of almost every description."

In the upstairs hall of Post's Algerita Hotel, Gladys encountered Gee McMeans, a former Texas Ranger and sheriff of Ector County who had married into the Sims family in 1905. Gladys and McMeans quarreled, then angrily produced pistols (proficient with handguns, Gladys preferred an automatic). Someone called down to the lobby, and within moments Sheriff E. J. Robinson and officer J. E. Cash hustled up to the second floor, where Gladys and McMeans were locked in a standoff, brandishing pistols while shouting at each other. Officer Cash asked Gladys to surrender her gun. When she refused, Cash tried to seize the weapon. Her gun went off in the sudden scuffle that followed. The bullet narrowly missed

The Algerita Hotel, scene of the 1916 confrontation between Gladys Sims and Gee McMeans, and their well-armed supporters. Later McMeans tried to goad an unarmed Harrison Hamer into a fight in the hotel.

(Photo by Karon O'Neal)

Cash, but Gladys dropped the gun and Sheriff Robinson quickly seized it. The hallway was crowded with members of both factions, but the sheriff and a few other peacemakers finally persuaded everyone to surrender their weapons. A small arsenal was collected: the guns of one faction were held in the First National Bank, while the weapons of the other group of partisans were placed in an office on the main street.[8]

The next morning, as everyone crowded into the courtroom, Sheriff Robinson conducted a search for concealed weapons. While Robinson checked the men, Miss Annie Rodgers (specially deputized for this task) examined Gladys and the eight or ten female witnesses.

Standing, from left, at the Johnson ranch house: Rubinelle "Dugie" Johnson, daughter of Emmett and Rocky and Pink's first grandchild; Beverly and Helen Trix Sims, daughters of Ed and Gladys.
(Courtesy Betty L. Giddens)

The court proceedings were peaceful, with Cullen Higgins contending that the divorce case should be considered in Scurry County, where Gladys had filed. The lawyer for Ed Sims countered that Post City was the rightful trial location, since the couple had made their home in Garza County. Proceedings were suspended, pending action of the Scurry County court, and by that evening Gladys and Ed Sims, along with their lawyers and friends, and guns, had left town.

The divorce was granted later in the year. But Gladys and Ed, and their families and friends, remained at odds over the custody of daughters Helen and Beverly. The frequent divorces of contemporary society produce countless conflicts and immeasurable antagonisms between parents over child custody. At least the fact that this wrenching problem is commonplace today is an initial step toward accommodation. In 1916, divorce was uncommon, and to the social stigma of legal division was added the unexpected pain of separation from children. In the months after their acrimonious divorce, Gladys and Ed Sims were jealous of the time spent with their

Post City

When Gladys and Ed Sims squared off against each other in Post in 1916, the seat of Garza County was less than a decade old. Post City was founded by cereal magnate C. W. Post, who had determined to create a model community in West Texas. Born in Illinois in 1854, Post was a successful salesman and inventor of agricultural machinery. Business ventures brought him to Texas in 1886. By the 1890s Post was suffering health problems from overwork, and he began experimenting with a cereal drink for himself that he labeled Postum. Soon he developed Post Toasties and Grape-Nuts, breakfast cereals that earned him a fortune.

Post was moved by the philanthropic impulses common to wealthy men of the era, deciding upon a West Texas colonization project that would offer families the opportunity to purchase homes or farms at low monthly payments. In 1906 Post bought 225,000 acres of land along the Caprock. The next year, when Garza County was organized in the vicinity, Post laid out a townsite near the center of the new county, and Post City became the county seat.

Post built a big department store and dozens of houses (one-, two-, three- and four-bedroom houses, beginning at $800). One of his favorite construction projects was the two-

(continued on next page)

daughters. The bitterness exploded with deadly effect in Snyder on Saturday, December 16, 1916.[9]

Ed Sims remarried shortly after divorcing Gladys. Gladys and her daughters stayed at the Johnson Ranch, but Ed frequently demanded custody of the girls. There was considerable conflict over custody times, and Sims came to feel that Gladys and her parents were "prejudicing his children against him." Ed freely expressed his bitterness; in later legal pro-

(continued from previous page)
story Algerita Hotel, which he provided with a chef, fine linens, and Post cereals on every breakfast table. He erected and equipped the region's finest hospital. Main Street was 120 feet wide, with grass, trees, and flowers planted in boulevard style. Post had high concrete curbs built, so that women could step easily from their carriages.

The town was surrounded by 160-acre farms, available from Post at generous terms, and by 1915, 300 farms had been sold. To provide adequate rainfall, Post tried seeding the clouds from firing stations along the rim of the Caprock. In 1912 alone more than 24,000 pounds of dynamite were detonated in generally unproductive attempts to produce rain. Post hired a geologist to locate oil, and he built an enormous cotton mill which would provide hundreds of jobs. He also had a recreational lake built near town, and Two Draw Lake became a regional oasis and the site of an annual Fourth of July celebration.

Sadly, Post's health failed in 1914, and he committed suicide at the age of fifty-nine. By then the town he had founded boasted over 1,000 residents, ten retail businesses, and three churches. After Post died his town commonly was called "Post," rather than "Post City." But a great many of the houses and commercial structures erected for Post City still stand, tributes to the philanthropic efforts of C. W. Post.

ceedings Cullen Higgins cited "a long series of insulting conduct" by Sims against Gladys and other members of the
Johnson family.[10]

Expecting a visit with his daughters to begin on Saturday,
December 16, Ed went to Snyder on Friday. About 9:30 that
evening at the Warren Drug Store, there was a scene with
Gladys' father Billy Johnson, witnessed by third parties, in
which Ed complained vehemently that Johnson and his wife
were trying to alienate the girls against their father. Ed, who
was a Garza County deputy sheriff, angrily pulled a gun, but
he was quickly disarmed by Scurry County Deputy Sheriff Sam
Casstevens. Two pistols were taken from Sims, and word
spread about the ugly confrontation. Later that night at the
ranch, Billy Johnson described the incident to his family, infu-
riating daughter Gladys and son Sidney.

On Saturday morning Sims sought out Scurry County
Sheriff W. A. Merrill, asking that he bring the girls into town
from the Johnson Ranch. Sheriff Merrill, attempting to avert
further conflict, warned Sims not to carry a pistol in Scurry
County unless on official duty, then asked Billy Johnson to
have the children brought into Snyder. Johnson agreed to
phone Gladys at the ranch, but asked the sheriff to "be present and try to keep down trouble." At about twenty minutes
before noon, Johnson called the ranch and persuaded Gladys
to bring the girls into Snyder. She said she would reach town
by 12:30 and come to her father's bank.

At the Johnson Ranch north of Snyder, Helen and Beverly
Sims reluctantly climbed into the back seat of their mother's
car with their suitcases. Gladys took her place behind the
wheel, packing her automatic in her purse. In Snyder, Sidney
Johnson, deadly furious that Ed Sims had pulled a gun on his
father, brought a pump action shotgun into the bank. Later
Sidney restlessly went outside to sit in his parked car. Then Ed
Sims drove up and parked in front of the bank. Ed and Sheriff
Merrill got out to wait for Gladys to arrive. Spotting Sidney in
his car, Sheriff Merrill asked him to go inside his father's

West side of the Snyder square, ca. 1910.
(Courtesy Scurry County Museum, Snyder, Texas)

bank. Saturday was the town's busiest day, but the square was even more crowded than usual with Christmas shoppers in their automobiles, wagons, and buggies.

Gladys drove onto the square at 12:30 and found a parking space near the bank. Ed and the sheriff went back to the Sims car, where Ed had stowed a .30-30 rifle, and drove back to within twenty feet of Gladys and the children. Ed walked over to the driver's side of the parked car, while the sheriff stood beside the left front fender. At the request of Sheriff Merrill, City Marshal O. P. Wolfe also was on hand to prevent hostilities. But there were not enough peace officers in Scurry County to head off what happened next.

Ed leaned into the car and kissed his daughters. While Gladys grumbled that she had brought the girls but would not make them go if they did not want to, Ed asked the children where their suitcases were. The girls said that their bags were beside them in the back seat, but that they were not going with him.

"Oh, yes," insisted Ed, "you must go with me." He reached inside the car, pulled out one of the suitcases, and placed it on the runningboard. The girls were crying that they were not going, so Ed grabbed Beverly, the youngest, and tried to pull her out of the car. Already seething, Gladys exploded when Ed seized her little girl.

She produced her automatic and, reaching across Beverly, triggered three rounds rapid-fire. The first bullet hit Ed's hat brim, "for I saw the fur fly," testified Sheriff Merrill.

"--- ---- you," growled Ed, grappling for the gun. Gladys got off a fourth round before the gun dropped behind the seat, and Sheriff Merrill pulled Ed away, intending to prevent him from going for his gun in his car.

Ed had been hit twice. A slug was lodged in his lower left leg, and another bullet had produced a flesh wound in the front of his chest. "You see what you have done," gasped Ed, "I am unarmed."

Billy Johnson barreled out of the bank to protect his

granddaughters, and Sidney Johnson suddenly stepped in front of the car with his shotgun. As Ed stumbled away from the car, Sidney's shotgun roared. The load of buckshot caught Ed beneath his right shoulder blade, and he collapsed onto his back.

Sidney pumped another round into the chamber, but Sheriff Merrill instantly leaped onto the sidewalk and seized the shotgun. Merrill handed the shotgun to Marshal Wolfe as Sidney muttered that "no man can curse my sister and her children" and "you cannot shoot and do around here like you can at Post City."

A large crowd of onlookers surged to the scene. Sheriff Merrill and a few other men carried Sims into Thompson's Drug Store, located almost directly in front of Gladys' car. Sims was placed on a table in the back room of the drug store, and Dr. W. R. Johnson was summoned. (Dr. Johnson was not related to Billy Johnson, but he was a friend of the family.) When Dr. Johnson arrived, Sims was struggling for breath, and within moments he died. The corpse was taken to an undertaker's office on the west side of the square, where Dr. Johnson and another physician conducted an examination. They ruled that the bullet wounds were superficial, but death had been inflicted by the shotgun blast. Justice of the Peace D. F. Wilson announced an examining trial for Monday afternoon, and placed Sidney Johnson under a $5,000 bond, which was readily posted by his father.

Many relatives and friends of Ed Sims journeyed south to Snyder when they heard of the killing. His body was taken back to Post, and a large crowd attended his funeral on Sunday. Feelings were ugly over the killing, and there were enough threats to prompt Sheriff Merrill to wire Governor James Ferguson a request "two experienced rangers. . . to remain through the Christmas holidays." Ranger Captain Joe Fox sent word that two of his men were on the way.[11]

Judge Cullen Higgins represented Sidney and Gladys at the examining trial on Monday. The State of Texas was repre-

The north side of the Snyder square, from a 1911 postcard. Cullen Higgins occupied upstairs offices in the First National Bank building on the corner. The double-parked car is about where Ed Sims double-parked on December 16, 1916, behind his ex-wife's car. Gladys shot him from her car, then Sid came from the bank and finished Ed with a shotgun.

(Courtesy Scurry County Museum, Snyder, Texas)

Interior of the First National Bank, with president Billy Johnson standing in front, wearing a bow tie and holding his big rancher's hat. (Courtesy Scurry County Museum, Snyder, Texas)

sented by County Attorney W. W. Weems and by J. Henry Beall, a former district judge from Sweetwater. The lengthiest testimony was given by Sheriff Merrill. Indictments were handed down, but Justice Wilson granted bail for Sidney for $20,000 and for Gladys for $8,000. "The bonds were immediately posted," reported the *Snyder Signal*, which published the testimony of the examining trial.

The Snyder newspaper also reflected the strong support of the community: "The Johnsons are a pioneer family and are among our most substantial citizenship. They own vast property interests here, being extensively interested in farming and ranching. W. A. Johnson is President of the First National Bank, and is an honorable, upright man. Sidney Johnson and Mrs. Sims have been reared here and have hosts of friends."[12]

Attorneys for the prosecution were justifiably concerned

Picnic Day on the Snyder square in 1912. The courthouse, where Sid and Gladys were examined in the shooting death of her ex-husband, was completed in 1911. Scurry County's original courthouse, a two-story brick structure, stands at far right.

(Courtesy Scurry County Museum, Snyder, Texas)

about the "hosts of friends" enjoyed by the Johnsons in Scurry County. The prosecution maneuvered to have the trials moved out of Scurry County, contending that it was not possible to seat an impartial jury in Snyder. Most potential jurors had read the testimony of the examining trial as published in the *Snyder Signal*; in case anyone had missed the newspaper account, a circular containing the testimony was printed and distributed throughout the region; and the Johnson family and Ed Sims were related to many members of the jury pool in Scurry and adjoining counties.

These arguments were presented to District Judge Warren Walter Beall in Snyder on June 7, 1917. Judge Beall ruled that a change of venue was needed in the interests of impartiality. Gladys would be tried at Lamesa, seat of Dawson County to the west, while Sidney would stand trial in Callahan County, in Baird, twenty miles east of Abilene. Bail for Sidney was $12,500, and among his eight sureties were his father, his brother Emmett, noted pioneer J. Wright Mooar, and a lawman of growing reputation, Frank Hamer.

During this troubled time Gladys and Texas Ranger Frank Hamer fell in love, and their marriage would add to the mounting turbulence.

10

Shootout in Sweetwater

"I got him! I got him!"

H. E. Phillips, after shooting at Frank Hamer

WHEN LAWMAN FRANK HAMER, a veteran of numerous violent encounters, married Gladys Johnson Sims, the Johnson faction acquired a formidable reinforcement. Francis Augustus Hamer was born on March 17, 1884. He was the second of eight children born to Frank and Lou Emma Francis Hamer. The senior Hamer was an ex-cavalryman who had served as a farrier with Col. Ranald Mackenzie and his famed Fourth Cavalry in Texas. Following his discharge, he married a Texas girl, and they would raise their family in San Saba and Llano counties. Young Francis (also called Frank or Pancho) learned his way around his father's blacksmith shop, and he grew up riding and roping, hunting and fishing. Francis reveled in the

132

outdoor life of the Texas Hill Country, but he was a bright grade school student, and in church services he developed the ambition to become a preacher.[1]

In 1900, however, the aspiring preacher clashed with a neighbor named Dan McSwain. Wounded from ambush by a shotgun blast, young Hamer nicked McSwain with a pistol bullet, then was carried to safety by his younger brother, Harrison. After healing from his buckshot wounds, sixteen-year-old Frank Hamer rode to the McSwain Ranch, then killed McSwain in a revolver duel. Soon afterward Frank and Harrison left home to seek work as cowboys. In 1905, while Frank was cowboying on a ranch near Fort Stockton, two rustlers stole horses from the spread. Within a few days Hamer, now an imposing 6'3 and 195 pounds, tracked down the rustlers and captured them at Winchester point. A few months later Hamer intercepted another rustler. He enjoyed the feeling of bringing criminals to justice, and in 1906 twenty-two-year-old Frank Hamer enlisted as a private in the Texas Rangers.

After two years of Ranger duty along the Rio Grande, Hamer was recommended for the post of city marshal of Navasota. Navasota was plagued by rowdy troublemakers and racial conflict, but Marshal Hamer vigorously exerted control. He had learned a rough brand of law enforcement from the Texas Rangers, and an anti-Hamer faction developed in town. But Hamer battled the lawless element in Navasota from 1908 until 1911, when he was hired as a special officer by Mayor Baldwin Rice of Houston.

Hamer rejoined the Texas Rangers in 1915, when Mexico was torn by revolution. He again was assigned to border duty, and there were vague rumors of violent encounters with smugglers and bandits. Frank Hamer became known as "a power for law and order," according to Texas Ranger historian Walter P. Webb.[2] In 1916, when the Texas Cattle Raisers Association asked the Texas Rangers to detach a man to help them apprehend rustlers, Frank Hamer was assigned to the association with a commission as a Special Texas Ranger.

ENLISTMENT, OATH OF SERVICE, AND DESCRIPTION RANGER FORCE.

Company ___C___ Ranger Force, Station ___Alpine Texas___

THE STATE OF TEXAS,
COUNTY OF ___Pecos___

I, ___Francis Augustus Hamer___, born in ___1884___ in the State of ___Texas___, aged ___22___ years and ___1___ months, and by occupation a ___Cow Boy___ do hereby acknowledge to have voluntarily enlisted this day of ___21 April___, 190_6_, as a private in the Ranger Force of this State, for the period of two years, unless sooner discharged by proper authority. And I do also agree to accept from the State of Texas such bounty, pay, subsistence and other expenses as are or may be established by law. And I do solemnly swear that I will faithfully and impartially discharge and perform all the duties incumbent on me as an officer of the Ranger Force according to the best of my skill and ability, agreeably to the Constitution and laws of the United States and of this State, and I do further solemnly swear that since the adoption of the Constitution of this State, I being a citizen of this State, have not fought a duel with deadly weapons, nor have I acted as second in carrying a challenge, or aided, advised or assisted any person thus offending. And I furthermore swear that I have not, directly nor indirectly, paid, offered or promised to pay, contributed nor promised to contribute, any money or valuable thing, or promised any public office or employment, to secure my appointment. So help me God.   ___F A Hamer___

Subscribed and sworn to before me this ___21___ day of ___April___ A. D. 190_6_.

___J B Husspeth justice of Peace and Ex officio notary public for Pecos County Texas___

I certify that ___F A Hamer___, the above named man, has been carefully examined by me previous to his enlistment and to the best of my knowledge and belief he is physically able, competent to and will faithfully perform the duties incumbent on him in accordance with law. This man is ___22___ years ___Blue___ months of age. Height ___6___ feet ___3___ inches. Complexion ___Light___ Eyes _____ Hair ___Brown___ Born at ___Fairview___ County of ___Wilson___ State of ___Texas___ Occupation ___Cow Boy___ Married or single ___Single___ Previous service ___None___

Remarks _____

___J H Rogers___
Captain Co ___"C"___ Ranger Force

Enlistment of Texas Ranger Frank Hamer.
(Courtesy Texas Ranger Hall of Fame and Museum)

By 1916 Harrison Hamer was cowboying for the Johnson Ranch north of Snyder. When a case brought Frank to Snyder, he went out to the ranch to see his younger brother. At the ranch Frank was introduced to Gladys Sims, who was deeply impressed by the big lawman. Gladys was embroiled in the most upsetting period of her life, and Frank Hamer was a tower of strength. A mutual attraction developed, and Frank and Gladys were married in New Orleans on May 12, 1917, shortly before her scheduled appearance before the district court. Frank became stepfather to Helen and Beverly Sims, and he would provide a strong masculine image for the girls. But his marriage to Gladys added Frank Hamer to the hit list of those who sought vengeance for the shooting death of Ed Sims.[3]

Frank Hamer, sitting tall in the saddle on a favorite horse, Bugler.
(Courtesy Texas Ranger Hall of Fame and Museum)

It was rumored that S. D. Sims, father of Ed, had hired gunmen to seek revenge against the Hamer brothers, Bill Johnson, Sheriff W. A. Merrill, and perhaps others. Hamer's biographer quoted Hamer family members who listed the assassins as Bob Higdon, H. E. Phillips, W. G. Clark, T. A. Morrison, and former law officer Gee McMeans, who had drawn a pistol on Gladys at the Algerita Hotel in Post during the volatile divorce proceedings of July 1916. At the same hotel, on a later occasion, Gee McMeans encountered Harrison Hamer, who still was cowboying for the Johnson Ranch. Harrison had left his weapons in his room, but McMeans was wearing a brace of revolvers, and he tried to goad the unarmed Hamer into a fight. Harrison wisely backed away while McMeans laughed provocatively.[4]

Frank Hamer did not know McMeans, but he announced "that if anyone murdered my brother that they would pay dearly for it. . . ." Frank then began to hear that McMeans was boasting "that he would kill me on sight. . . ." Frank took the precaution of carrying around an even larger arsenal than usual. On a September morning he rode into Snyder from the Johnson Ranch with Harrison and Billy Johnson. At a distance from the road, the party sighted a wolf and stopped the car. Frank stepped out with a rifle and opened fire at the wolf on a distant horizon.[5]

Suddenly, four men jumped up from a point of conceal-ment between the car and the wolf. These gunmen had set an ambush beside the ranch road, but apparently thought that the lethal Frank Hamer somehow had spotted them and had begun shooting at them. They sprinted to their car and sped away toward Snyder. The Johnson car followed, and in town Frank and Harrison recognized two of the bushwhackers passing in front of the First National Bank. The two brothers manhandled both men, cuffed them around, and challenged them to fight with pistols, but they offered no resistance and were allowed to retreat.

A few weeks later, at nine o'clock on Monday morning,

October 1, 1917, Sidney Johnson was scheduled for trial in Baird. Cullen Higgins, insisting that he needed Gladys Hamer as a witness for Sidney, managed to have charges reduced from murder to assault with intent to kill, and to have her case brought to court in Lamesa on Monday, September 17. Although the trial packet is missing from the courthouse in Lamesa, volume one of the *Criminal File Docket* and volume one of the *District Court Criminal Minutes* reveal that Cullen persuaded the district attorney to drop the charges against Gladys. The record of Cullen's legal arguments is unavailable, but it had to be persuasive that Gladys was the only surviving parent of two young girls (whose new stepfather was the widely respected Frank Hamer); the bullets she fired did not produce the fatal wounds; and she was a female in 1916 Texas.[6]

Gladys, therefore, was able to come to Baird on October 1, along with her husband, his brother Harrison, her brother Emmett, and dozens of other witnesses subpoenaed to

Sidney Johnson was held in the Callahan County Jail during his trial in Baird. The venerable jail is still in use.   **(Photo by Karon O'Neal)**

"personally appear" at Sidney Johnson's trial. Among others called were Sidney's father, Emmett's wife, Gladys' daughters, and Bill Wren, along with Gee McMeans, Bob Higdon, and Si Bostick. A special venire of forty-eight potential jurors also assembled. But the day's proceedings quickly ended, "continued by agreement" until the fall term.[7]

Gladys' daughters apparently returned to Snyder with their grandfather and aunt, perhaps by train. Gee McMeans and other assassins hurried ahead to set an ambush in Sweetwater, fifty miles west of Baird. Frank, Gladys, Harrison, and Emmett piled into a car to drive back to Snyder. Frank Hamer had been tipped off that Gee McMeans and other hired gunmen were planning an attack. A southpaw, Frank had his .45 ("Old Lucky") strapped on his left hip, but he belted on another handgun, a Smith and Wesson .44, as a backup.

The party reached Sweetwater about half past one in the afternoon. Driving in from the east past the tall Bluebonnet Hotel, Frank headed for a garage on the southeast corner of the square to have a punctured tire repaired. Gladys stayed in the car while Harrison and Emmett went to find a toilet and Frank walked to the office.

Gee McMeans had spotted his prey, and when Frank emerged from the office Gee jumped from a doorway and leveled a .45 automatic. McMeans fired at pointblank range, and the heavy slug slammed into Hamer's left shoulder. McMeans was exultant, "I've got you now, God damn you!"[8]

Hamer instantly took a swipe with his right hand at the .45 automatic, knocking it downward just as McMeans again pulled the trigger. The second bullet tore into Hamer's right thigh. Ignoring his wounds, Hamer gripped the barrel of the automatic, tore it from the fist of McMeans, then began pounding his assailant with his right hand.

While Hamer struggled with McMeans, H. E. Phillips advanced across the street with a shotgun. Seeing another gunman approach her husband from behind, Gladys screamed out a warning, then produced her automatic. Gladys opened fire, driving Phillips behind a parked car. He tried to advance again, but once more she sent him back to cover. Phillips swung his shotgun toward Gladys, then ducked behind the car as she continued to fire.

When Gladys ran out of bullets, Phillips hurried over to the two men grappling in front of the garage. McMeans twisted free from Hamer's grip, and Phillips loosed a shotgun blast at the tall lawman's head. Buckshot cut off Hamer's hat brim.

"I got him! I got him!" shouted Phillips.

Hamer sank to his knees, then began shaking his head from the ear-splitting report of the shotgun. Realizing that Hamer was not dead, McMeans pulled out a pump shotgun, but Hamer had drawn and aimed the .44 Smith and Wesson. Although forced to shoot with his right hand, Hamer drilled McMeans through the heart.

The Bluebonnet Hotel stood half a block east of the square in Sweetwater. On October 1, 1917, a grand jury was meeting in the hotel because the new courthouse (seen with white columns left of center) was still under construction. When a gun battle broke out at the southeast corner of the square (left edge of photo at center), grand jury members looked out to view the action. **(Courtesy Pioneer Museum, Sweetwater)**

McMeans dropped dead on the sidewalk beside the car. The fight suddenly left Phillips, who dropped down beside his dead comrade. Hamer limped over and, seeing that Phillips still had a shotgun, challenged him to shoot it out. But Phillips suddenly scrambled up and ran away, still carrying the shotgun.

Frank would not shoot Phillips in the back, but Harrison emerged from the toilet, seized a rifle, and darted into position to fire at his brother's assailant. Frank knocked the barrel up as Harrison pulled the trigger, and Phillips ducked into the side door of a cafe. Harrison gave chase, but when he peered into the cafe from the doorway he could not see Phillips, who was flattened behind the door. Although Harrison went back to help his brother, Phillips was arrested a short time later by a deputy sheriff. A policeman intercepted a woman on the street with a paper sack containing $5,000 in ten-dollar bills, money intended for the assassins.

A new courthouse was under construction on the Sweetwater town square, and the county had rented rooms in the Bluebonnet Hotel for official purposes. The hotel overlooked the scene of the shootout. A grand jury was meeting in the hotel, and when the jury members heard gunfire they hurried to the windows.

It was customary in the Old West that following a fatal shootout a coroner's jury of witnesses immediately would assemble. If the victim had been armed, the jury would rule that the shooting had been self-defense, which would conclude the legal proceedings almost before the gunsmoke had cleared.

Early in the twentieth century, West Texans still were connected in spirit, custom, and outlook to the Old West. The Sweetwater grand jury members invited Frank Hamer, a tough lawman they deeply respected, to join them for a prompt legal closure to the shootout. While a doctor began to work on Frank's wounds, the grand jury stated that they had witnessed the encounter and that Hamer had shot McMeans in self-defense. The grand jury no-billed Hamer, and commended him

for resisting the temptation to shoot Phillips in the back. With
the legal action now finished, Frank retired to submit to more
thorough medical treatment.

Within a few hours Bob Higdon arrived on the train in
Sweetwater, walking downtown just in time to see a corpse
being carried to the undertaker. Assuming that the body
beneath the shroud was Frank Hamer, Higdon crowed loudly
that he had planned to kill the officer and that McMeans
should have waited for him. Finally he was told that Hamer
had killed McMeans, and although wounded, Frank was still
in Sweetwater. Sobered by the death of his fellow assassin,
Higdon muttered something about not taking advantage of a
wounded man, then he left town on the next train.

Frank Hamer had been shot twice with a .45. When he
was able to travel, Frank and Gladys and their daughters journeyed to California, where Billy Johnson owned a house. While
recovering from his wounds, Frank met Tom Mix and other
Western movie actors, and in future years Mix would visit the
Hamers in Texas. On April 11, 1918, the Hamers welcomed a
new member of the family, Frank, Jr. And because of his
lengthy recuperation in California, Hamer would be absent
from the next round of violence in West Texas.[9]

11

Murder in Clairemont

"You mentioned Judge Higgins.
Now there was a great man."

Lena Hopson Powell

THE KILLING OF GEE MCMEANS by Frank Hamer was a set-back to the plans for vengeance for the death of Ed Sims. But the setback proved only temporary, as more gunmen were hired and an even more vicious murder was planned. Judge Cullen Higgins had represented Gladys Sims in her divorce from Ed Sims, then he had been instrumental in clearing Gladys and her brother, Sidney Johnson, of all charges in Ed's shooting death. Furthermore, as a special prosecutor, Higgins was preparing a murder case for the pending trial of Will Luman, who was free on bail and who had his own obvious reasons to see Cullen dead. A respected jurist and lawyer,

142

widely admired as a churchgoing family man, Higgins was unaware that he was being stalked by assassins.

On Sunday, March 17, 1918, Cullen Higgins taught his boys' Sunday school class, then attended morning services at the Methodist Church in Snyder. The next day district court would open at Clairemont, the seat of Kent County, and Higgins was involved in several cases. On Sunday afternoon, therefore, he bade farewell to his wife and little boy, then traveled, apparently by automobile, to Clairemont, thirty-five miles to the northeast.

Clairemont was established in ranching country in 1888, and the little town was designated county seat when Kent County was organized in 1892. Lumber was hauled in from Snyder, and building stone was quarried from Butte Knob east of Clairemont. A two-story red sandstone courthouse was completed in 1895, and a jail of the same material was erected to the east. By 1918 the population of Clairemont was two hundred, with several businesses, a hotel, and a newspaper clustered near the courthouse, along with a school and a church.

Cullen Higgins built this home for his family in 1917, but he would live in it only a short time before he was murdered.   **(Photo by Karon O'Neal)**

In 1893 red sandstone was quarried east of Clairemont for the construction of a two-story courthouse. Today there is only one story, and the county seat was moved to Jayton in 1954.   **(Photo by Karon O'Neal)**

A red sandstone jail was built in Clairemont just east of the courthouse. Both structures stand vacant today.   **(Photo by Karon O'Neal)**

The church was holding a revival in March 1918, and when Cullen Higgins arrived from Snyder he attended Sunday evening services. Higgins then went to the hotel, where he sat in the lobby conversing with his successor as district judge, John B. Thomas, and a court reporter named Wiess. While these men talked, assassins crept up to a window overlooking the lobby. One of the hired killers leveled a shotgun, then triggered a load of buckshot into the back of Cullen Higgins.[1]

As the assassins fled, the stricken man was carried to his bed. A telephone message brought a number of Snyder friends, who took Olive Higgins to Cullen's bedside. It was decided to move him to "a sanitorium" at Spur, about twenty miles to the north. At Spur a doctor extracted five buckshot, but two other slugs could not be found, so internal surgery was performed early Monday afternoon. When it was revealed that his intestines had been punctured, his wife and friends feared the worst. On Tuesday, Higgins was conscious, and he told those at his bedside that he was ready to go. Cullen Higgins died at twenty minutes past noon that day. Only forty-two, he had survived his father by merely three and a half years.

Judge Higgins was one of the most prominent and admired men in the region. The Masonic Lodge of Spur formed a procession to escort the body twenty miles toward Snyder, and another procession brought Higgins to his new home. The funeral was conducted on Wednesday afternoon, with every business in Snyder closed for the occasion. Although West Texas was sparsely settled, a crowd of two thousand assembled, including friends from New Mexico, Oklahoma, and Colorado. Cullen's brother, Tom Higgins, came by train from Lampasas. Tom now was a lawyer and a judge, but he packed a pistol, in case he might need to defend himself. Religious services were conducted by two ministers at the Methodist Church, followed by the Masonic funeral ritual at the Snyder Cemetery north of town.

On the night that Cullen Higgins was shot, the court reporter, Wiess, recognized Si Bostick on the porch of the

The courthouse in Clairemont in its original form. The man at upper right is perched on the second-floor porch of the hotel, northeast of the courthouse, where Cullen Higgins was assassinated.

(Courtesy Betty L. Giddens)

Clairemont Hotel. Bostick and the other assassins sprinted away from the hotel on foot, then mounted up and galloped west out of town. Learning from Wiess about the presence of Si Bostick, the sheriff at Clairemont telephoned the sheriff's office at Post, where Bostick made his home with a wife and three children.

Texas Rangers Sam McKenzie and H. L. Koons, stationed in Sweetwater, went to Post to search for Bostick. He was not at home, of course, but the Rangers initiated a search of the countryside. On Tuesday at midday—during the very hour that Cullen Higgins died—the Rangers arrested Bostick at the ranch of Tom Askins, about twelve miles north of Post. Bostick was jailed at Post, but feelings were so high that the next day McKenzie and Koons spirited their prisoner to an unknown destination. Late Wednesday night the Rangers hustled Bostick into a third-floor cell at the red brick jail on the courthouse square in Sweetwater.

The impressive headstone of Cullen Higgins' grave is shaded by a tree in the Snyder Cemetery.   **(Photo by Berri Hodges)**

The old Nolan County Jail stood on the northeast corner of the square in Sweetwater. Confined here after his arrest as a suspect in the murder of Cullen Higgins, Si Bostick was found dead in his cell.

(Courtesy Pioneer Museum, Sweetwater, Texas)

Law enforcement officers of this era routinely used harsh methods to extract information from prisoners. Bostick provided the names of his accomplices, Bob Higdon and Will Luman, and on Thursday they were arrested in Post. Incarcerated under heavy guard in Snyder, within a few days they were moved to the jail in Anson, then transferred to more secure confinement in Fort Worth. Security was a priority, because by this time Si Bostick had been found dead in his cell.

On Friday morning, March 22—Bostick's second morning in the Sweetwater jail—Deputy Sheriff T. B. Thompson approached the third-floor cell with breakfast. Bostick did not answer the deputy's greeting. Thompson peered into the cell, then dashed out to find the sheriff.

The sheriff, county health officer, and other officials soon crowded into the cell to examine Bostick's lifeless body. His belt was fastened around his neck and connected by a torn strip of bedsheet to a bar on the window. A pocket handkerchief was stuffed into his mouth. It was determined that he had been dead for several hours. His neck was not broken, and he was leaning against the wall—with his bare feet touching the floor. The newspaper headline proclaimed that the prisoner "HANGS SELF IN HIS CELL," and speculated that he had drawn "the strap around his neck taut enough to induce death by choking." An inquest was promptly held, and Justice of the Peace John Bryan ruled that Bostick's death "was self-committed by hanging."[2]

It strains belief that a man with his feet touching the floor would lean hard enough and long enough against a belt noose to kill himself by slow strangulation. It also was thoughtful of him to stuff a handkerchief into his mouth to muffle any outcry, particularly since no other prisoners were nearby.

Although it was dubious that Si Bostick killed himself in such an excruciatingly improbable manner, there had been no lynch mob. The public was unaware of his presence in Sweetwater. But law officers knew where Bostick was held, and they were bitter over the cold-blooded murder of a respected former judge. There were rumors that Rangers had slipped into Bostick's cell, and Higgins descendants still believe—approvingly—that lawmen killed Bostick.

Certainly it would not have been unusual in 1918 for officers to visit a prisoner's cell for heavy-handed interrogation. If an accused murderer later was discovered hanged, other officials might easily suggest suicide in order to protect officers who had provided a rough measure of justice. There are no official documents about Bostick's hanging, only a newspaper account which describes an unlikely "suicide."

The day after the hanging, several lawmen went to a stock tank between Clairemont and Post in search of the murder weapon. Among the officers were brothers Frank and Nath (short for Nathan) Terry, first cousins of Cullen Higgins and both future sheriffs of Fisher County. Nath Terry stripped off his clothes and dove into the frigid water. Soon he emerged with a shotgun which belonged to Si Bostick, who had insisted

Nath Terry and his wife, Jessie. Nath found the shotgun used in the murder of Cullen Higgins, and later he became sheriff of Fisher County.

(Courtesy Bob Terry)

that Bob Higdon pulled the trigger in Clairemont. It seems highly coincidental that the murder weapon, discarded in a stock tank, was located the day following Bostick's death. A reasonable assumption might be that Si Bostick told about the shotgun and everything else they wanted to know to nocturnal visitors who were threatening to hang him.[3]

Bob Higdon and Will Luman were indicted for the murder of Cullen Higgins. Higdon was thought to have fired the fatal blast, but Si Bostick would prove to be the sacrificial goat for justice. The identical indictments charged that Higdon (and Luman) did "advise, command and encourage the said Si Bostick to do and commit the said murder, the said R. N. Higdon [and Will Luman] not being personally present when said offense was committed by the said Si Bostick."[4]

Once it was stated legally that Higdon and Luman were not present when Cullen Higgins was murdered, then it was "agreed by the attorneys representing the state that the case is a bailable one." Judge Thomas set bail at $10,000 for each defendant. Four friends combined to post $10,000 for the release of Will Luman, while S. D. Sims, Sr., was one of two men who pledged "their land, tenements, [and] goods chattels" for Bob Higdon's bond. The general view was that Higdon had fired the fatal blast into Cullen Higgins, and that he had been hired by Sims to avenge the death of his son, while Luman was along for his own reasons.[5]

At the September 1918 term of the district court in Clairemont, Judge Thomas ruled that the trials of Higdon and Luman should be moved from Clairemont, the site of the murder, to the November district court term in Haskell. The trials were postponed, but in April 1919 Luman was declared guilty of manslaughter and sentenced to five years in prison. The verdict was appealed, and Luman seems later to have won

Sheriffs

An unusual number of men involved in the events of this book were selected, at one time or another, to hold the prestigious and hazardous office of county sheriff. Pink's father-in-law, Albertus Sweet, was sheriff of Lampasas County for five years during the 1870s. N. O. Reynolds, who helped to quell the Horrell-Higgins violence as a Texas Ranger, settled in Lampasas and was elected sheriff in 1886. Pink's lifelong friend, Bill Wren, served a four-year term as Lampasas County sheriff during the 1890s.

Gee McMeans, who pulled a gun on Gladys Johnson Sims in 1916 and who was killed by Frank Hamer in 1918, was a former sheriff of Ector County. A decade before his fatal gunfight with Pink, Bill Standifer was sheriff of Crosby County. The Terry brothers—Nath, who found the shotgun used to murder Cullen Higgins, and Frank, who was rumored to have been in the Sweetwater jail when Si Bostick hanged himself— both went on to serve as sheriff of Fisher County.

Although Pink Higgins was never a county sheriff, he must have been gratified to hold a deputy sheriff's commission in Kent County during the latter years of his life.

release. Higdon never stood trial for the death of Joshua Bostick, and after various legal delays neither Higdon nor Luman was tried for the murder of Cullen Higgins.

Higdon, apparently retiring from the hired killer business, permanently assumed a low profile. A few years after standing trial for the murder of Joshua Bostick and Cullen Higgins, Luman was employed as an undercover man by the Texas and Southwestern Cattle Raisers Association. Later he was promoted to inspector, and he worked for the association for many years. Luman died at the age of eighty-six in 1977, widely respected for his long career in law enforcement.[6]

On Monday, April 1, 1918, two weeks after the shooting of Cullen Higgins, Sidney Johnson reappeared—with new counsel—in court at Baird. Once more the case was continued, to September 23, 1918. Following the murder of Johnson's attorney, the case attracted even greater attention then before. A special venire of seventy-two men produced a jury, and proceedings began on September 23 before Judge Joe Burkett. Two days later the jury returned a verdict of not guilty.[7] The testimony has disappeared from among the documents in the trial packet at the courthouse in Baird, just as Gladys Hamer's trial packet at Lamesa's courthouse and all documents concerning the death of Si Bostick in Sweetwater have vanished. Other legal materials regarding the events of this turbulent period likewise cannot be found. An investigator is tempted to conclude that in 1918 some prominent individual used his influence to obtain official documents that might reflect badly upon his family or friends.

Sidney Johnson divorced, remarried, and spent his life as a prosperous rancher noted for an explosive temper. He was killed when he was struck by a car in San Antonio in 1959. Sidney was sixty-nine, and he was buried in Snyder. His petite and feisty sister, Gladys, found a fine match in her second husband. Gladys and Frank Hamer were happily married for thirty-eight years, making their home in Austin until Frank died in 1955 at the age of seventy-one. Hamer's splendid career as a law officer was capped in 1934, when he led the manhunt which resulted in the deaths of Bonnie and Clyde.[8]

Emmett Johnson was generally considered the most genial of the Johnson siblings. A lifelong rancher, he enjoyed many friends and was a devoted member of the Methodist Church. Emmett and Rocky Higgins Johnson had two children (a third died in infancy), but he was accidentally killed in 1927, during the twentieth year of their marriage. Although she had a formidable temper, Rocky was strong-minded and enterprising. To sustain herself in widowhood, she established a successful truck farm in the Rio Grande Valley. She also engaged in real estate, wrote for a newspaper, and toyed with the notion of producing a book about Pink. Late in life Rocky became convinced that "Gladys and Sid planned for weeks to murder Ed," she wrote her daughter. "Up to that time Gladys and I were always very friendly. I never could stand her after that."[9] Rocky also was frequently, but affectionately, judgmental about two of her sisters, Ruby and Nell.

Ruby married Dixie Smith, but she was widowed at a relatively young age, and she did not prove as successful as Rocky at supporting herself. Nell wed J. W. Henry and stayed in Spur, helping to care for the crippled Rena and for her mother. But Henry put Rena to work in his store, a property he persuaded his mother-in-law to acquire for him.

Following the accidental death of her husband, Rocky Higgins Johnson supported herself with various enterprises. Rocky's correspondence to her children sheds considerable light on the life of her father. **(Courtesy Betty L. Giddens)**

Nell taught music and long served as the principal musician of the First Methodist Church of Spur. Bonnie married Baxter Scoggins, and they made their home in Ada, Oklahoma.[10]

Tom Higgins served a total of sixteen years as Lampasas County judge, the longest tenure of any man to hold the position. Judge Higgins was a noted community leader, and so was his son, John T. Higgins, who also served as county judge, from 1954 to 1962.[11] Olive Higgins, Cullen's widow, married Rev. A. W. Waddill, who was the pastor of Snyder's First Methodist Church, and who officiated at Cullen's funeral. Rocky always felt that Olive was more compatible with her second husband than with Cullen. When Reverend Waddill died in 1939, Rocky pointed out to her daughter that several of his pallbearers also had been pallbearers for Cullen. "Snyder men will get tired of carrying her husbands out, I fear."[12]

Although the participants are gone now, there are many tangible reminders of the Higgins world. In Lampasas the Star Hotel and a few other structures from the 1870s still stand. The picturesque courthouse was erected in 1883, and a number of other limestone buildings that Pink would recognize from the 1880s and 1890s are around or near the square. Higgins Gap continues to be a landmark in northern Lampasas County. Pink's parents and other relatives are buried at rural Rock Church Cemetery, while two or more of the Horrell brothers lie side by side in Oakwood Cemetery in Lampasas.

Clairemont is a ghost town, but the deserted jail and part of the courthouse remain from the community's violent past. In Snyder the old First National Bank building still stands at the northwest corner of the square; Cullen Higgins kept his law offices upstairs, and Ed Sims was killed nearby. Cullen's "new" house is still inhabited in Snyder, and the magnificent Johnson ranch house continues to command a ridge ten miles north of town. Cullen rests in the Snyder Cemetery, along with Rocky and Emmett Johnson, and numerous other relatives. Pink and Lena, who died in 1937, are interred at the Spur

The old Star Hotel is one of several Higgins-era structures still standing in Lampasas. On the morning of June 7, 1877, Pink, Bob Mitchell, Bill Wren, and Bob Terry passed the hotel, riding left to right, moments before falling under fire. **(Photo by Karon O'Neal)**

The old First National Bank building, on the northwest corner of the Snyder square. The law office of Cullen Higgins was upstairs.
(Photo by Karon O'Neal)

Cemetery, and the foundation of their house can be located in the harsh country where they made their last home. Pink's final victim, Billy Standifer, is buried in one of the loneliest gravesites in the West.

Standifer's gravestone announces that he was "KILLED BY PINK HIGGINS." But Standifer had tried to kill Pink. Standifer then met the same fate as many other men who demonstrated deadly intentions toward Pink, who pragmatically felt that the country was better off without each of the hardcases who fell before his guns. Ironically, the intended accusation on Standifer's gravestone provides instead a fitting tribute to one of the most courageous and effective of all Western gunfighters.

⊙ Endnotes ⊙

CHAPTER 1: A Half Century of Higgins Violence
1. Charles Adam Jones, "Pink Higgins, The Good Bad Man." *Atlantic Monthly* (July 1934), pp. 88-89.

CHAPTER 2: Early Life of Pink Higgins
1. Genealogical information in this chapter was provided to the author by Dr. John Higgins of Lampasas, including photocopies of pertinent pages of the old family Bible.

2. When Mary Higgins died in 1883, it was stated that she was "114 years, 5 months, and 5 days" of age, the oldest person in the state." If this calculation was correct, then she was fifty-four when she gave birth to John Holcomb Higgins, Pink's father. Whatever her age, she was buried in the family cemetery near Higgins Gap.

3. Census statistics were given to the author on a handout by Dr. James V. Reese of Stephen F. Austin State University.

4. Charles Adam Jones, "Pink Higgins, The Good Bad Man." *Atlantic Monthly* (July 1934), p. 85.

5. Lampasas County Historical Commission, *Lampasas County, Texas*, p. 1.

6. The history of Fort Gates and Fort Croghan is detailed in Hart, *Old Forts of the Far West*, pp. 16-21.

7. Charles Adam Jones, "Pink Higgins, The Good Bad Man." *Atlantic Monthly*, p. 85.

8. Clifford B. Jones, "Notes on the Life of 'Pink' Higgins," p. 2.

9. The gravestone of John Higgins states that he was a private in the 27th Brigade. The history of the 27th and the other frontier units is detailed in Smith, *Frontier Defense in the Civil War*. "Military Activities" in Lampasas County are described in *Lampasas County, Texas*, p. 17.

10. Brown, *Indian Wars and Pioneers of Texas*, pp. 114-115.

11. *Lampasas County, Texas*, pp. 18-20.

12. *Austin Daily State Journal*, August 15, 1870.

13. *Lampasas County, Texas*, pp. 19-20.

14. *Ibid.*, p. 20.

15. *Lampasas County, Texas*, p. 418; Clifford B. Jones, "Notes on the Life of 'Pink' Higgins," p. 3.

16. Clifford B. Jones, "Notes on the Life of 'Pink' Higgins," pp. 3-4.

17. *Ibid.*, pp. 4-5.

18. *Ibid.*, p. 5.

19. *Lampasas Leader*, July 27, 1934; *Lampasas County, Texas*, pp. 368-370.

20. Clifford B. Jones, "Notes on the Life of 'Pink' Higgins," p. 2; *Lampasas Leader*, July 27, 1934.

21. Clifford B. Jones, "Notes on the Life of 'Pink' Higgins," p. 2.

22. *Lampasas County, Texas*, p. 209.

23. Information about Betty Mitchell and her family is available in *Lampasas County, Texas*, pp. 209 and 281.

CHAPTER 3: The Horrell Brothers

1. A mine of information about the Horrells was compiled by Frederick Nolan in *Bad Blood: The Life and Times of the Horrell Brothers*.

2. John Nichols, interview by J. Evetts Haley (May 15, 1927), pp. 6, 42, 43.

3. *Ibid.*, p. 43.

4. *Ibid.*, pp. 6-7; Frederick Nolan, *Bad Blood*, pp. 11-12.

5. Nichols interview, pp. 42-43.

6. *Ibid.*, pp. 7-8.

7. Accounts of the encounter between Williams' force and the Horrells are in Gillett, *Six Years with the Texas Rangers*, pp. 73-75, and the Nichols interview, pp. 7-9.

8. Gillett, *Six Years with the Texas Rangers*, p. 74.

9. *Ibid.*, p. 75; Frederick Nolan, *Bad Blood*, pp. 27-28.

10. The story of the Horrell War is detailed in Rasch, "The Horrell War," and Frederick Nolan, *Bad Blood*, pp. 47-95.

11. Gillett, *Six Years with the Texas Rangers*, p. 77; Lampasas County Historical Commission, *Lampasas County, Texas*, p. 24.

CHAPTER 4: The Horrell-Higgins Feud

1. Shootouts in early Lampasas are described by Jeff Jackson in articles published in the Lampasas County Historical Commission's *Lampasas County, Texas*, pp. 24-28.

2. John Nichols, interview by J. Evetts Haley, p. 16.

3. *Lampasas Leader*, January 26, 1889.

4. Nichols interview, p. 10.

5. Sonnichsen, *I'll Die Before I'll Run*, pp. 135-136; Douglas, *Famous Texas Feuds*, pp. 136-137.

6. Nichols interview, p. 22.

7. *Ibid.*

8. *Ibid.*, p. 10.

9. Sonnichsen, *I'll Die Before I'll Run*, p. 136.

10. Nichols interview, pp. 13-14; Gillett, *Six Years with the Texas Rangers*, p. 77.

11. Frederick Nolan, *Bad Blood*, pp. 112 and 115; *Lampasas County, Texas*, p. 26.

12. *Lampasas Leader*, January 26, 1889.

13. Clifford B. Jones, "Notes on the Life of 'Pink' Higgins," p. 8.

14. Askins, *Texans, Guns & History*. This book is unreliable on a great many points, but it would be intriguing to learn the source of Askins' stories about Terrell and Lantier, as well as the two-day siege. According to Askins, Terrell was the rustler that Pink shot and stuffed into a freshly butchered beef, creating the miracle of "a cow giving birth to a man." Askins said that Pink encountered Lantier at a water hole. Lantier went for his revolver, but Pink already had unsheathed his Winchester and drilled him in the belly. The two-day siege, unreported in any other source, could have been based on some sniping incident during what the Lampasas Leader (January 26, 1889) called "guerrilla warfare."

15. Clifford B. Jones, "Notes on the Life of 'Pink' Higgins," pp. 8-9.

16. Nichols interview, p. 23.

17. Jeff Jackson has conducted the most detailed historical study of the battle in Lampasas, presenting his findings in *Lampasas County, Texas*, p. 26, and in an excellent brochure, "Historical Guide to the Shootout on the Public Square." A thorough account which rings with the authority of eyewitnesses was published twelve

years after the shootout, in the *Lampasas Leader* (January 26, 1889). Also see the eyewitness description by John Nichols on pp. 11-12 and 23-24 of his interview by J. Evetts Haley.

18. Nichols interview, pp. 11-12.

19. *Ibid.*, pp. 11 and 23.

20. *Lampasas Leader*, January 26, 1889.

21. Nichols interview, p. 24.

22. *Lampasas Leader*, January 26, 1889.

23. *Ibid.*

24. Maj. John B. Jones to Adjutant General William Steele, July 10, 1877.

25. Contemporary accounts of this daring and bloodless arrest are available in Gillett, *Six Years with the Texas Rangers*, pp. 78-79, and *Roberts, Rangers and Sovereignty*, pp. 167-169. The *Lampasas Leader* (January 26, 1889) account was based on eyewitnesses, and C. L. Sonnichsen, *I'll Die Before I'll Run*, pp. 140-142, interviewed family members.

26. Gillett, *Six Years with the Texas Rangers*, p. 79.

27. *Ibid.*, p. 80.

28. Both letters are reproduced in Webb, *Texas Rangers*, pp. 335-338.

CHAPTER 5: Aftermath of a Range War

1. The Story of the murder and lynching at Meridian may be studied in: John Nichols interview by J. Evetts Haley, pp. 25-26; Sonnichsen, *I'll Die Before I'll Run*, pp. 147-149; Frederick Nolan, *Bad Blood*, pp. 136-150; Jackson, "Vigilantes: The End of the Horrell Brothers," *NOLA Quarterly* (April-June 1992), pp. 13-19. Jeff Jackson, who has accumulated more information about this period of Lampasas County history than any other investigator, believes it likely that Pink and Bob Mitchell were involved in the lynching of Mart and Tom Horrell.

2. Jeff Jackson related the murders of James Collier, Bill Vanwinkle, and William Kinchelo in Lampasas County Historical Commission, *Lampasas County, Texas*, p. 27. Also see Frederick Nolan, *Bad Blood*, pp. 150-152.

3. Russell, *Bob Fudge*, pp. 20-23, 41.

4. Jones, "Notes on the Life of 'Pink' Higgins," pp. 12-13.

5. *Lampasas Leader*, April 6, 1882; *Galveston Daily News*, April 15, 1882.

6. Jeff Jackson learned from Higgins family members the circumstances of Betty's affair and departure.

7. *J. P. Higgins vs. Delilah E. Higgins*, in *Lampasas County District Court Minutes*, Vol. 4, p. 235.

8. Jeff Jackson compiled the history of Albertus Sweet in "Victim of Circumstance: Albertus Sweet, Sheriff of Lampasas County, Texas, 1874-1878," *NOLA Quarterly*, Vol. 20, pp. 14-21. Lena's birthdate is inscribed on her tombstone in the Spur Cemetery. Jackson quotes the census that Lena was ten in 1870. But if Lena was born in 1860 (instead of 1868), her mother would have been only eleven when giving birth.

9. Jones, "Notes on the Life of 'Pink' Higgins," p. 4.

10. The account of this incident was drawn from documents about Case No. 1268, *The State of Texas vs. J. P. Higgins*, Lampasas County District Court. Copies of these documents were provided to the author by Jeff Jackson.

11. Russell, *Bob Fudge*, p. 20.

12. Jones, "Notes on the Life of 'Pink' Higgins," pp. 10-11. Historians at the Whitehead Memorial Museum in Del Rio could uncover no accounts in local sources of an 1880s fight involving Pink Higgins, but they suggested that this lack of records certainly did not preclude that some sort of clash had occurred.

13. Interview with Jeff Jackson, September 29, 1998.

14. J. P. Higgins, Certificate of Prison Conduct, December 3, 1893.

15. *Ibid.*

16. Dr. John Higgins of Lampasas told the author about the sojourn in East Texas during which Cullen and Tom Higgins attended business colleges. Tom's obituary lists his matriculation at Tyler Commercial College and at "summer normals" for teachers.

17. Dr. Sonnichsen related his experiences in Lampasas to the author in 1987 and 1988.

18. Dr. John Higgins offered the author these conclusions about Cullen's preparation for the bar.

CHAPTER 6: Spur Ranch Range Wars

1. My grandmother, Mrs. W. W. Standard, and mother, Jessie Standard O'Neal, provided information about the move of Jess Standard. Billy Standifer and his father are described in Lampasas County Historical Commission, *Lampasas County, Texas*, p. 350; Billy's activities as a cowboy are mentioned in Hunter, *The Trail Drivers of Texas*, pp. 345-346; Billy's tenure as sheriff of Crosby County was related to me by Verna Anne Wheeler of the Crosby County Pioneer Memorial Museum in Crosbyton. The Rasberry and

Higdon families are mentioned in *Lampasas County Cemeteries*, pp. 254 and 264.

2. Bill Wren's term as sheriff is listed in *Lampasas County, Texas*, p. 420. The Terry move to Roby is detailed by their grandson, Bob Terry.

3. The definitive account of the Spur Ranch is Holden, *The Espuela Land and Cattle Company*. The Spur correspondence and financial records are deposited at the Southwest Collection on the campus of Texas Tech University.

4. Holden, *The Espuela Land and Cattle Company*, pp. 209 and 213.

5. Melton, "Recollections of Tom Horn."

6. Spur Records, Vol. X, p. 29.

7. Spur Records, Vol. VIII, p. 374.

8. Spur Records, Vol. X, p. 225.

9. Rocky Higgins Johnson to her daughter, "Dugie" Johnson Miller, May 12, 1942; Spur Records, Vol. X, pp. 613-614.

10. Spur Records, Vol. X, pp. 613-614; Clifford B. Jones, "Notes on the Life of 'Pink' Higgins," p. 14; Elliott, *The Spurs*, pp. 123-124.

11. Charles Adam Jones, "Pink Higgins, The Good Bad Man," *Atlantic Monthly* (July 1934), 87.

12. Spur Records, Vol. X, pp. 613-614.

13. *Ibid*.

14. Charles Adam Jones, "Pink Higgins, The Good Bad Man," *Atlantic Monthly*, 88; and Spur Records, Vol. X, pp. 613-614.

15. Charles Adam Jones, "Pink Higgins, The Good Bad Man," *Atlantic Monthly*, 88.

16. In his article for *Atlantic Monthly*, Charles Jones described the fight "in Higgins's own words, just as he often told it to me." Clifford Jones, in "Notes on the Life of 'Pink' Higgins," related an identical version, as told to him by his father and by Pink. W. J. Elliott, in his book *The Spurs*, pp. 122-127, offers the same version, along with a statement signed by Mrs. Lena Higgins in the town of Spur on January 25, 1936: "I find it to be a true and correct account of the incidents that led up to the tragedy."

17. Charles Adam Jones, "Pink Higgins, The Good Bad Man," *Atlantic Monthly*, 88.

18. Spur Records, Vol. X, pp. 613-614.

19. Charles Adam Jones, "Pink Higgins, The Good Bad Man," *Atlantic Monthly*, 88.

CHAPTER 7: Pink's Final Years

1. Holden, *Espuela Land and Cattle Company*, pp. 217-218.

2. Kent County Court, In the Matter of J. P. Higgins, Deceased, January 2, 1914.

3. Details about John Snowden and Jeff Hardin were related to the author by Kennith Hardin of Rotan.

4. *The Texas Spur*, December 26, 1913.

5. Charles Adam Jones, "Pink Higgins, The Good Bad Man," *Atlantic Monthly* (July 1934), pp. 88-89.

6. O'Connor, *Wild Bill Hickok*, p. 96.

7. Kelton, *Elmer Kelton Country*, p. 133.

8. *Lampasas Leader*, January 15, 1904.

9. Descendants have provided the author with information about John and Hester Higgins, and birth and death dates are on their gravestones in Rock Church Cemetery.

10. Sinise, *Pink Higgins*, p. 43.

11. Kelton, *Elmer Kelton Country*, p. 133.

12. *The Texas Spur,* December 26, 1913.

CHAPTER 8: A New Round of Violence Begins

1. Case No. 497, District Court of Kent County. *State of Texas vs. Si Bostick* for cattle theft.

2. Case No. 166, District Court of Kent County. *State of Texas vs. Lee Rasberry* for cattle theft. There are 130 pages of testimony, which provide most of the details used by the author in describing this incident.

3. Case No. 166, p. 39.

4. Case No. 3291, Texas State Court of Appeals. Appeal from Jones County, Lee Rasberry, Appellant. *Abilene Reporter*, March 6, 1916.

5. The long-told story about Rasberry writing Sid Johnson and Joshua Bostick was related to me by Kennith Hardin of Rotan and Bob Terry of Roby, who also both described to me the subsequent shooting in Rotan.

6. Case No. 820, District Court of Fisher County. *State of Texas vs. Will Luman* for murder, p. 113.

7. *Ibid.*, pp. 113-114.

8. *Ibid.*, p. 120.

9. *Ibid.*, p. 121.

10. Luman "Trailing Up Cow Thieves," Part I, *The Cattleman* (April 1978), p. 86.

11. Case No. 820, p. 117.

12. *Ibid.*, p. 123.

13. *Abilene Reporter*, March 6, 1916; *Snyder Signal*, March 10, 1916. These two newspapers offered accounts of the shooting and aftermath, in addition to the accounts in the lengthy trial testimony.

14. The two-year history of the case against Rasberry and Luman may be traced through the numerous documents in the file of Case No. 820. Luman's arrest is described in the *Snyder Signal* of May 18, 1917, and in his testimony in Case No. 820.

CHAPTER 9: Death in Snyder

1. The background of Pete Snyder and the town he founded is related in Charles G. Anderson (ed.), *Reflections, An Album of West Texas History, 1840-1990*, pp. 109-118.

2. Pritchett and Black, *Kent County and Its People*, p. 204.

3. *Snyder Signal*, March 22, 1918.

4. Holt, *The District Courts of Scurry County and Their Presiding Judges*, "Judge Cullen C. Higgins."

5. Information about the Johnson family was obtained from the obituaries of W. A. Johnson in the *Scurry County Times* (January 22, 1931), Nannie Sims Johnson in the *Scurry County Times* (May 19, 1927), and Sidney A. Johnson in the *Snyder Daily News* (July 31, 1959). Also see Parks and Cramer, eds., *First Cattlemen On the Lower Plains of West Texas*, pp. 13-17.

6. *Scurry County Marriage Record Book I, 23 August 1884 to 19 April 1907*, p. 17; Betty Giddens to the author, August 24, 1998.

7. *Sweetwater Daily Reporter*, July 31, 1916.

8. The armed encounter in Post is decribed in a *Post City Post* article reprinted in the *Sweetwater Daily Reporter*, July 31, 1916.

9. The killing of Ed Sims is described in the *Snyder Signal* (December 22, 1916), and testimony in the subsequent examining trial is printed verbatim in this same issue.

10. Case No. 644, District Court of Scurry County. *State of Texas vs. Sidney Johnson* for murder.

11. The telegram is quoted in the *Snyder Signal*, December 22, 1916.

12. *Snyder Signal*, December 22, 1916.

CHAPTER 10: Shootout in Sweetwater

1. For background on Frank Hamer see Frost and Jenkins, *"I'm Frank Hamer," The Life of a Texas Peace Officer*. Also see file on

Hamer at the Texas State Historical Association in Austin and at the Texas Ranger Hall of Fame Library in Waco. A lengthy phone interview with Frank Hamer, Jr., produced rich information about Frank and Gladys Hamer from their son.

2. Webb, *The Texas Rangers*, p. 546.

3. Frost and Jenkins, *"I'm Frank Hamer,"* pp. 66-67.

4. *Ibid.*, pp. 67-68.

5. *Ibid.*, pp. 68-70.

6. Case No. 645, District Court of Scurry County. *State of Texas vs. Sidney Johnson* for murder. Case No. 140, District Court of Dawson County. *State of Texas vs. Gladys Sims* for assualt with intent. Criminal Minutes, District Court, Dawson County, vol. I.

7. Case No. 1794, District Court of Callahan County. *State of Texas vs. Sidney Johnson* for murder.

8. Frank Hamer, Jr., assured the author that the street fight in Sweetwater occurred exactly as described in *"I'm Frank Hamer,"* pp. 70-73.

9. Frank Hamer, Jr., related to the author details of the sojourn in California.

CHAPTER 11: Murder in Clairemont

1. The *Snyder Signal*, March 22, 1918, related a thorough account of the death and burial of Cullen Higgins. Later editions described the arrests of Si Bostick, Bob Higdon, and Will Luman.

2. *Sweetwater Daily Republic*, March 23, 1918.

3. Pink Terry related to Bob Terry and to the author, among others, the discovery of the shotgun.

4. District Court Records of Kent County: Indictments of R. N. Higdon and Will Luman, Grand Jury, Special Term, March 1918.

5. District Court Records of Kent County: R. N. Higdon, Habeas Corpus application, May 3, 1918; Cause No. 246, *State of Texas vs. R. N. Higdon*, September 23, 1918; Case No. 247, *State of Texas vs. Will Luman*, September 23, 1918.

6. District Court Records of Haskell County: Case No. 1157, *State of Texas vs. Will Luman*, November 12, 1917–May 22, 1919; Case No. 1233, *State of Texas vs. Will Luman*, May 5, 1919–December 10, 1919; Case No. 1234, *State of Texas vs. R. N. Higdon*, May 5, 1919–December 10, 1919. For background on Luman and his later life see Luman, "Trailing Up Cattle Thieves," *The Cattleman* (April and May 1978).

7. Case No. 1794, District Court of Callahan County. *State of Texas vs. Sidney Johnson* for murder.

8. The *Snyder Daily News* reported Sidney's death and summed up his career in the July 31 and August 2, 1959, issues. Also see the article on Sidney in Chamblin, ed., *The Historical Encyclopedia of Texas*, p. 1061. The lives of Gladys and Frank Hamer are described in Frost and Jenkins, *"I'm Frank Hamer."* Frank Hamer, Jr., also provided the author with information about his parents.

9. Rocky Higgins Johnson to her daughter "Dugie" Johnson Miller (November 2, 1952). As the years passed, Rocky's correspondence (1932–1954) revealed numerous unpleasantries about Sidney and Gladys (it is not known how they felt about Rocky). Emmett's lengthy and informative obituary was published in the *Snyder Signal*, May 19, 1927. I am indebted to Betty Giddens for correspondence, obituaries, and many other materials about her grandparents that she made available to me.

10. I was able to piece together information about Ruby, Nell, Rena, and Bonnie primarily from the correspondence of Rocky Higgins Johnson (1932–1954).

11. Dr. John T. Higgins of Lampasas graciously provided me with a great deal of material about his grandfather, Tom Higgins. Also see Lampasas County Historical Commission, *Lampasas County, Texas*, pp. 208, 420.

12. Rocky Higgins Johnson to Dugie Johnson Miller (March 14, 1939).

◉ Bibliography ◉

Documents

Callahan County District Court Records, Baird, Texas.

Dawson County District Court Records, Lamesa, Texas.

Fisher County District Court Records, Roby, Texas.

Haskell County District Court Records, Haskell, Texas.

Higgins, J. P. Certificate of Prison Conduct (December 3, 1893). Texas State Archives, Austin.

Jones County District Court Records, Anson, Texas.

Kent County District Court Records, Jayton, Texas.

Kent County Court. In the Matter of J. P. Higgins, Deceased (January 2, 1914).

Lampasas County District Court Records, Lampasas, Texas.

Scurry County District Court Records, Snyder, Texas.

Scurry County Marriage Record Book I, 23 August 1884 to 19 April 1907. Snyder, Texas.

Books

Anderson, Charles G. *Reflections: An Album of West Texas History 1840-1990*. Snyder, Texas: Scurry County Historical Commission, 1990.

Askins, Col. Charles. *Texans, Guns, & History*. New York: Winchester Press, 1970.

Brown, John Henry. *Indian Wars and Pioneers of Texas*. Austin, Texas: L. E. Danniell, Publisher, 1880.

Chamblin, Thomas S., ed. *The Historical Encyclopedia of Texas*. Austin: The Texas State Historical Institute, n. d.

Douglas, C. L. *Cattle Kings of Texas*. Austin, Texas: State House Press, 1989.

————. *Famous Texas Feuds*. Dallas, Texas: Turner Company, 1936.

Elliott, W. J. *The Spurs*. Spur, Texas: Publishers, The Texas Spur, 1939.

Elzner, Jonnie. *Relighting Lamplights of Lampasas County*, Texas. Privately published, 1974.

Frost, H. Gordon, and John H. Jenkins. *"I'm Frank Hamer," The Life of a Texas Peace Officer*. Austin and New York: The Pemberton Press, 1968.

Galusha, Bill. *C. W. Post, The Man—The Legend*. Slaton, Texas: Brazos Offset Printers, Inc., n. d.

Garavaglia, Louis A., and Charles G. Worman. *Firearms of the American West, 1866-1894*. Albuquerque: University of New Mexico Press, 1985.

Gard, Wayne. *Frontier Justice*. Norman: University of Oklahoma Press, 1949.

Gillett, James Buchanan. *Six Years with the Texas Rangers*. New Haven: Yale University Press, 1925.

Griswold, J. T. *From Dugout to Steeple*. N. p.: J. T. Griswold, 1949.

Hart, Herbert M. *Old Forts of the Far West*. Seattle, Washington: Superior Publishing Company, 1965.

Holden, William Curry. *The Espuela Land and Cattle Company*. Austin: Texas State Historical Association, 1970.

Holt, Wayland G. *The District Courts of Scurry County and Their Presiding Judges: The First One Hundred Years*. Snyder, Texas: Scurry County Historical Commission, 1985.

Hunter, J. Marvin. *The Trail Drivers of Texas*. Austin: University of Texas Press, 1922.

Kelton, Elmer. *Elmer Kelton Country, The Short Nonfiction of a Texas Novelist*. Fort Worth: Texas Christian University Press, 1993.

Lampasas County Historical Commission. *Lampasas County Cemeteries, 1856-1995*. Austin, Texas: Eakin Press, 1995.

Lampasas History Book Committee, compilers. *Lampasas County, Texas, Its History and Its People*. Marceline, Missouri: Walsworth Publishing Company, 1991.

Nolan, Frederick. *Bad Blood: The Life and Times of the Horrell Brothers*. Stillwater, Oklahoma: Barbed Wire Press, 1994.

Nunn, W. C. *Texas Under the Carpetbaggers*. Austin: University of Texas Press, 1962.

O'Connor, Richard. *Wild Bill Hickok*. New York: Ace Books, Inc., 1959.

Parks, Aline, and Dudley Cramer, eds. *First Cattlemen On the Lower Plains of West Texas*. Snyder, Texas: Ranch Headquarters Association, 1971.

Pritchett, Jewell G., and Erma Barfoot Black. *Kent County and Its People*. Rotan, Texas: Rotan Advance Newspaper Office, 1983.

Roberts, Capt. Dan W. *Rangers and Sovereignty*. San Antonio, Texas: Wood Printing & Engraving Co., 1914.

Russell, Jim. *Bob Fudge, Texas Trail Driver, Montana-Wyoming Cowboy, 1862-1933*. Aberdeen, South Dakota: North Plains Press, 1981.

Sandoz, Mari. *The Cattlemen*. Lincoln: University of Nebraska Press, 1958.

Shelton, Hooper, compiler. *History of Scurry County, Texas, From Buffalo . . . to Oil*. Snyder, Texas: Feather Press, 1973.

Sinise, Jerry. *Pink Higgins: The Reluctant Gunfighter*. Quanah, Texas: Nortex Press, 1974.

Smith, David Paul. *Frontier Defense in the Civil War*. College Station: Texas A & M University Press, 1992.

Sonnichsen, C. L. *I'll Die Before I'll Run*. New York: The Devin-Adair Company, 1962.

Webb, Walter P. *The Texas Rangers*. Austin: University of Texas Press, 1935.

Articles

Harton, Harold. "An Early-Day Incident with the 1873 Winchester .44.-40." *Lampasas Dispatch Record* (September 2, 1996), p. 6.

"History of the Horrell-Higins War, A Bloody Relic of By-Gone Days in Lampasas County." *Lampasas Leader* (January 26, 1889).

Holden, W. C. "The Problem of Stealing on the Spur Ranch." *West Texas Historical Association Year Book*, vol. VIII (June 1932), pp. 25-42.

———, ed. "A Spur Ranch Diary, 1887." *West Texas Historical Association Year Book*, vol. VII (June 1931).

Jackson, Jeff. "Victim of Circumstance: Albertus Sweet, Sheriff of Lampasas County, Texas, 1874-1878." *Quarterly of the National Association for Outlaw and Lawman History*, vol. XX, no. 3 (July-September, 1996), pp. 14, 16-21.

———. "Vigilantes: The End of the Horrell Brothers." *NOLA Quarterly*, XVI, no. 2 (April-June 1992), pp. 13-19.

Jay, Don M. "Bad Blood." *Frontier Times* (January 1967), pp. 16-17.

Jones, Charles Adam. "Pink Higgins, The Good Bad Man." *Atlantic Monthly* (July 1934), pp. 79-89.

Kinney, Harrison. "Frank Hamer, Texas Ranger." *The American Gun* (February 1961), pp. 82-89.

Luman, Bill (Dutch), as told to Jane Pattie. "Trailing Up Cow Thieves," Parts I and II. *The Cattleman* (April 1978), p. 40 ff., and (May 1978), p. 56 ff.

Rasch, Philip J. "The Horrell War." *New Mexico Historical Review*, vol. 31, no. 3 (July 1956), pp. 223-231.

Rylander, Dorothy. "The Economic Phase of the Ranching Industry in the Spur Ranch." *West Texas Historical Association Year Book*, vol. 7 (June 1931), pp. 56-67.

Newspapers

Abilene Reporter

Austin Daily Journal

Galveston Daily News

Lampasas Dispatch News

Lampasas Leader

Scurry County Times

Snyder Signal

Sweetwater Daily Reporter

The Texas Spur

Miscellaneous

Correspondence between Rocky Higgins Johnson and her children, 1932-1954. Betty L. Giddens, Fort Worth.

Correspondence between Rocky Higgins and Emmett Johnson, 1905-1907. Betty L. Giddens, Fort Worth.

Jones, Clifford B. "Notes on the Life of 'Pink' Higgins." Unpublished typescript.

Jackson, Jeff. "Historical Guide to the Shootout on the Public Square." Lampasas, Texas: 1990.

Melton, Henry. "Recollections of Tom Horn." Typescript on file at Wyoming State Historical Society, Cheyenne.

Nichols, John, interview by J. Evetts Haley (May 15, 1927). Haley Library and History Center, Midland, Texas.

Price, Margaret Ann. *From Rails to Rigs: The Early History of Ector County, Texas, 1881-1927*. Master's Thesis, University of Texas Permian Basin, 1977.

Spur Ranch Records, Vol. X, Correspondence, 1899-1903. Southwest Collection, Texas Tech University, Lubbock, Texas.

◉ Index ◉

171